GEORGIA IN THE WAR
1861-1865

A Compendium of Georgia Participants
by
Charles Edgeworth Jones

of Augusta, GA

Formerly, Historian of
Camp No. 435, U.C.V.

GEORGIA MILITARY HISTORY SERIES

Foote & Davies
Atlanta, GA
1909

FREEDOM HILL PRESS, INC.
Jonesboro, GA
1988

To the Memory of my parents,
This Book is lovingly inscribed.

-C.E.J.

For in our Cause, let none forget
Were Right and Truth conjointly met;
The hallow'd luster of our Creed
Is heightened as the Ages speed.

-C.E.J., 1899

Dedication of the Freedom Hill Edition

This volume, the third in our Georgia Military History Series, rightly should have been the first, for it is a basic reference which can be used while reading any of the volumes which have come before or those which will follow it. We feel that it is a valuable addition to the series and we hope that those who collect and read our volumes will find themselves referring to it again and again.

But aside from being a compendium of Georgia's war personalities, it is a concise and interesting historical work in itself. From these bits of Georgia history we receive a glimpse of our turn-of-the-century ancestors' self-image. We sense a proud people whom defeat has only tempered, and whose past is viewed without shame. It is to these stern and stalwart Georgia men and women, those who died for the Cause, and those who survived to reap the whirlwind following it, that this humble effort is dedicated. May a just Providence see that they rest in peace.

Allan and Frankie Heath
Freedom Hill Press
Jonesboro, GA
1988

Acknowledgments

Freedom Hill Press wishes to thank the Georgia Department of Archives and History, and especially its Assistant Director, Mr. Anthony Dees, for the loan of the rare first edition of this work. Mr. Dees, a true scholar and Southern gentleman, has, over the last few years, also become our friend.

Allan and Frankie Heath
Freedom Hill Press, Inc.
1988

"By the heavy guns at Pensacola, Mobile, and New Orleans,—behind the parapets of Pulaski, McAllister, and Sumter,—among the volcanic throes of Battery Wagner,—at Ocean Pond and Honey Hill,—upon the murderous slopes of Malvern Hill,—behind the lethal shadows of the Seven Pines,—in the trenches around Petersburg,—amid the smoke and carnage of Manassas, Fredericksburg, Spottsylvania, Chancellorsville, Sharpsburg, Gettysburg, Brandy Station, Cold Harbor, the Wilderness, Corinth, Shiloh, Vicksburg, Perryville, Murfreesboro, Missionary Ridge, Chickamauga, Franklin, Nashville, Atlanta, Jonesboro, Bentonville, and until the last thunders of war were hushed at Appomattox and Greensboro when, in the language of the present gallant chief magistrate of this commonwealth (Gen. John B. Gordon,—1886-1890), our regiments, brigades, divisions, and army corps were 'worn to a frazzle,' these brave Georgians were found shoulder to shoulder with heroic companions in arms, maintaining the honor of their State, and supporting the flag of their beleaguered country. You can mention no decisive battle delivered, no memorable shock of arms during the protracted and herculean effort to achieve the independence of the South, where Georgia troops were not present. Their life blood incarnadined, their valor glorified, and their bones sanctified the soil above which the Red Cross, which they had followed so closely, waved long and fearlessly in the face of desperate odds. All honor to the courageous men who fell in the forefront of battle. All honor to the cause which enlisted such sympathy, and evoked such proofs of marvelous devotion. Precious for all time should be the patriotic, heroic, and virtuous legacy bequeathed by the men and the aspirations of that generation. Within the whole range of defensive wars you will search in vain for surer pledges and higher illustrations of love of country, of self-denial, of patient endurance, of unwavering confidence, and of exalted action."

(Colonel Charles C. Jones, Jr., LL.D.,—1889).

CONTENTS

PRELIMINARY STATEMENT.

Georgia was one of the original thirteen States, but was settled later than the others. The patent for it was granted to Oglethorpe, and other Trustees, June 9, 1732. The first colony, consisting of 120 persons, came in 1733; the objects of the colony being to establish a barrier between the Spaniards and Indians, on the south, and South Carolina and North Carolina on the north, and to provide a refuge for the honest-minded needy and destitute; especially, poor debtors, orphans, and friendless children and youth—the last-mentioned object being that of Whitefield.

The colony was at first military, and the colonists received their lands on condition of military service. This occasioned discontent, and many of them moved to North Carolina. The policy was changed, and 50 acres of land was offered, unconditionally, to all settlers; and many Scotch and German emigrants came in.

In the war between Great Britain and Spain in 1739-43, Oglethorpe attacked the Spaniards in Florida in 1740, but the expedition was a failure. The Spaniards attacked Georgia in 1742, but, becoming alarmed at Oglethorpe's stratagems, they returned to Florida. After the peace, Georgia demanded the slaves which had been prohibited to them, and in 1752 the trustees surrendered the colony to the crown and negro slavery was permitted.

While Georgia was not suffering as were the other colonies from British oppression, she made common cause with them in the Revolutionary War.

By the conclusion of a treaty of peace with the Creek and Cherokee Indians in 1791, the Creeks in 1802 ceded to the United States a large section of country in the southwestern section, and Georgia, in turn, relinquished to the United States all her claims west of the Chattahoochee, which surrender includes the present States of Alabama and Mississippi.

In 1860 this commonwealth followed the lead of South Carolina, and passed an Act of Secession, January 19, 1861.

Georgia repealed the Act of Secession, October 30, 1865, and adopted a new constitution, ratifying the Thirteenth Amendment; but congress, not satisfied with the constitution, put the State under military rule and another constitutional convention was called, which formed the constitution ratified in 1868. The State was restored to the Union on its ratification of the Fourteenth Amendment; but, on its refusal to ratify the Fifteenth Amendment, was again put under military rule.

On compliance, however, with this demand, it was re-admitted.

Joseph E. Brown was governor of the State from 1857 to 1865, and James Johnson provisional governor a part of 1865.

Alexander H. Stephens, of Georgia, was vice-president of the Confederate States.

Robert Toombs, of Georgia, became the first secretary of state of the Confederate States, February 21, 1861. He was afterwards a brigadier-general in the Confederate army.

SKETCH OF HISTORY OF GEORGIA. (1732-1909.)

Georgia was founded by James Edward Oglethorpe in 1733, the charter establishing it having received the Royal sanction June 9th of the previous year. The point selected for the first settlement was Yamacraw Bluff, on the right bank of the Savannah River. It was called Savannah after the stream which flowed by it; and the primal landing of the emigrants at their future home occurred on February 1, 1733. Tomo-Chi-Chi, Mico of the Yamacraws, who lived there, was a warm friend of Oglethorpe; and, from the first, he assisted him materially in the work of colonization.

One of the earliest acts of the founder, after the arrival of his colonists, was to define the outlines of his proposed Savannah. Through the industry of all concerned, the requisite clearing rapidly progressed, houses gradually supplanting tents, and soon the straggling settlement began to wear the aspect of a fully-fledged village. Early in the following year, Oglethorpe conscious of the dangers to which the English were exposed from their Spanish neighbors, and wishing to ascertain the possibilities of internal defense, projected a tour to the southern confines of the province. The trip was fruitful of good results, as the site of historic Frederica on St. Simon's Island, was then chosen. Almost coincidently with this visit, accessions were made to the little colony through the advent of the Salzburgers, the Moravians and the Highlanders. The last-named were valuable citizens from the start, and were always ready to take up arms for their beloved Georgia.

In the fall of 1735 the town of Augusta, on the Savannah River, was founded. It was, in its incipiency, and, for many years afterwards, a Trading-Post, and much business was transacted there. Its situation was an advantageous one. About this time, Oglethorpe made a trip to England and secured the needed reinforcements for Frederica. He was always thinking of the Spanish storm which was liable, sooner or later, to break upon his settlement. On his return he brought with him Charles Delamotte, a school teacher, and the brothers, John and Charles Wesley, to Savannah. Delamotte opened the first school for white children in the colony. John Wesley had the honor of introducing the pioneer Sunday-school into Georgia, and perhaps also the world. He was a remarkable divine.

In May, 1738, Oglethorpe was appointed general and commander-in-chief of His Majesty's forces in Georgia and South Carolina. As such he was instructed to inquire particularly into the designs, preparations and movements of the Spaniards in Florida. While his mind was intent upon these matters, he was apprised that the Red Men were soon to hold an important convocation at Coweta Town. This was to occur in July of the following year, and he realized how indispensable it was that he should attend. And so, with a few companions, he made the hazardous march of three hundred miles through the trackless wilderness, and appeared at the gathering. His admirable conduct appealed most strongly to the assembled braves, who discovered in him a worthy, fashioned in accordance with their highest ideals. About the same time, news was brought that the first overt act of Spanish aggression had been committed, and that English blood had been shed on Georgia soil. Accordingly, General Oglethorpe, in retaliation for this outrage, determined to lead a military expedition against St. Augustine. The expedition, however, through non-concert of action on the part of some of the troops, was destined to disappointment.

This was in the spring of 1740; and, two years later, in revenge for the attempted invasion of Florida, the Spaniards sent a monster Armada consisting of fifty-six sail, and conveying perhaps six thousand men, to sweep Georgia from the map. It was a case of history repeating itself. The undaunted resistance they met with everywhere, was but a grim foretaste of the humiliating Waterloo they were soon to encounter. In front of Frederica and indomitable Saint Simon's Island, the second Spanish Armada was baffled just as the first had been overwhelmed in the British Channel. Seldom was a defeat more crushing, or a victory more complete.

In July, 1743, General Oglethorpe bade a sorrowful and fatherly adieu to Georgia and set sail for England, never again to return. For a decade, or more, the colony was then subject to the rule of presidents. In 1754 it became a province of the Crown, and was placed under the domination of Royal Governors. There were three of these: Captain John Reynolds and Henry Ellis, Esq., being the first two. The third and perhaps the greatest of the gubernatorial trio was James Wright, Esq. (afterwards Sir James Wright) who, entering office in October, 1760, for two decades and more had a notably eventful administration. While he was a locum tenens, the Revolution began, and Governor Wright was responsible for preventing the colony from declaring itself until all of her other American sisters had spoken. True to his convictions, and at all times faithful to his beloved Sovereign, he was pre-eminently a courageous executive; and when the patriotic tempest did break upon his devoted head, it was beyond his power to control it.

In January, 1776, the Second Provincial Congress was triumphantly convoked at Savannah. An important feature of its work was the choice of five delegates for the Philadelphia conclave. Three of these deserve special mention as they had the honor of signing the Declaration of Independence. They were Button Gwinnett, Lyman Hall and George Walton. Now that Georgia had unqualifiedly placed herself in the Revolutionist column, the "Liberty Boys" were zealous in doing everything possible to put her in military condition. To this end, they gave their constant attention to raising and equipping companies and procuring supplies of arms and ammunition. In the latter connection they made valuable captures. Part of the gunpowder taken in one expedition, as tradition has it, was used at the Battle of Bunker's Hill. To cap the climax and show their utter contempt for the King, these undaunted Americans made his accredited representative, Governor Wright, a prisoner in his own home. The first noteworthy Revolutionary affair on Georgia soil occurred late in December, 1778. Savannah, then, fell into the hands of the British. This loss was a disastrous one, and, nine months later, an attempt was made by the combined French and American armies to retake the town. A desperate but fruitless assault was made in October, 1779, which resulted in much carnage. In the same year occurred the famous victory of Kettle Creek. It was a partisan triumph; as was also the siege of Augusta in the summer of 1781. A twelve-month later, Savannah was, without a struggle, surrendered to General Anthony Wayne by the English, and the war was over so far as Georgia was concerned.

After the restoration of peace, the work of rehabilitation occupied some time. The founding of the State University was one of the first useful things attempted. This was in 1783. Five years later, Georgia was admitted into the Union. January 2, 1788, was the exact date. About that time the Yazoo agitation began. It enlisted public attention until the famous overthrow of the accursed fraud in February, 1796. Early in the following century (1802), the commonwealth effected a sale to the General Government of her immense western territorial possessions. The consideration involved was one million, two hundred and fifty thousand dollars; and thus was a death-blow forever dealt to the Yazoo transaction.

The next exciting episode was the second war with England. That was in 1812-15. Only slight skirmishes occurred within the confines of the State. Then came Governor Troup's administration, and his historic clashes with Federal authorities; and, soon after, the removal to the West of the Creek and Cherokee Indians. Railroad building was now the problem of the hour; the succeeding decades showing great activity in that department. In the midst of all this internal development, news was brought of the opening of Mexican hostilities. Enthusiasm was widespread. Companies were formed and equipped, and, for months, everyone was thinking of those who had been sent to the front. Many Georgians won distinction in that conflict, It was the training-school for that larger struggle, soon to be introduced.

Everything now hastened to a finale. The next three terms must be passed over, and then we will come to the administration of Joseph E. Brown. It was, in many respects, a remarkable one. Commencing in 1857, during the eight years of its continuance, it was crowded with exciting events. Governor Brown was distinctively a self-made statesman. His indomitable will-power was the keynote of his success. He may have made mistakes, but he showed himself a man at all times.

For several years prior to the war between the sections, there were many premonitions of the approaching catastrophe. The rumblings of slave agitation were heard throughout the country—in congress and elsewhere. They delivered to the South a message which she could not ignore. Her States Rights doctrines, her private interests and everything she held sacred, were at stake, and she was forced to declare herself. This she did through her Secession Ordinances. In them she claimed the prerogative of withdrawing from the Union whenever she so desired. The first Southern State to take action in that important regard was South Carolina. This was in December, 1860. About a month later, or on the 16th of January, 1861, the famous Georgia convention was assembled. Its deliberations were destined to be fraught with mighty consequences. The contending forces in the gathering were almost equally matched; the secessionists slightly preponderating. But the Unionists made up in brilliant advocates, what they lacked in numbers, and, for three days and more, there was a death-grapple between the opposing contingents. The secessionists, too, had impassioned oratorical supporters, among whom was the gallant Thomas R. R. Cobb. He fell in battle, a brigadier-general, and an early sacrifice to the cause of Confederate liberty. It was his lot to make the pivotal speech of the convention. As a result of his burning appeal, it was decided on January 19, 1861, by a vote of two hundred and eight to eighty-nine, to adopt the Georgia Secession Ordinance.

From now on, war was the all-engrossing question. No stone unturned, the united effort was to develop the full military potentialities of the commonwealth. Young and old, from the first, contributed their patriotic mead. Georgia has every reason to feel proud of her courageous sons. The Augusta Powder Works was a monument to one of them (Col. (Gen.) George W. Rains). He has the distinction of having erected and successfully operated this gigantic plant. First and last, nearly three million pounds of gunpowder were manufactured within its imposing confines. It was indeed a bulwark of the beleaguered Confederacy.

The first noteworthy passage at arms on Georgia soil occurred in the spring of 1863. This was General Forrest's pursuit of Col. Streight's daring cavalry raid. The pursuit was a successful one, and resulted in a complete victory for General Forrest. Streight's entire command was captured. A few months later, the great battle of Chickamauga was fought. It lasted two days and was a most bloody and formidable engagement. Catoosa County, near the Tennessee border, was its scene. One hundred and thirty thousand men, all told, participated in the lethal struggle; the casualties amounting to nearly a fourth of that number. Generals Braxton Bragg and Rosecrans were the opposing generals.

May 4th, 1864, was the historic date when the great Dalton-Atlanta campaign was commenced. It was a tactical encounter. General Joseph E. Johnston with fifty thousand troops was in constant collision with General Sherman's splendidly equipped and numerically powerful army. It was another instance, in a way, of the Hammer and Rapier policy. General Johnston was continually falling back, exchanging one position for another, but fighting always. It was a masterly retreat which cost Sherman many of his men. His antagonist suffered far less. The sanguinary battle of Kennesaw Mountain was the principal one along the line of march. Three weeks later, General Johnston was summarily supplanted by General John B. Hood. The wisdom of the change may be questioned. General Hood was not the tactician his predecessor was, and Sherman apparently realized it at once. The former believed in aggressive warfare. A series of engagements around Atlanta soon followed. Though gallantly contested, they did not yield the wished-for fruits. Within a few weeks, Atlanta fell into the hands of the enemy.

Atlanta being captured, General Sherman decided to make his celebrated "March to the Sea." The movement was commenced about the middle of November, 1864. His army consisting, we are told, of sixty-five thousand veteran campaigners, met with little opposition to its triumphal progress. In fact, as Georgia was practically defenseless, only slight skirmishes, at best, were possible. The Federals were at liberty to devastate ad libitum. They are said to have cut a swath of sixty miles in width through the heart of the State. When Savannah was reached, the city was surrendered to Sherman without a struggle. It had been fortified with a view to standing a protracted siege. The next affairs within the borders of the commonwealth were those at West Point and Columbus, April 16, 1865. Desperate but ineffectual resistance was offered at both places. General R. C. Tyler held the Confederate fort at West Point. These were, it is said, the last battles of the war, east of the Mississippi River. The final melancholy happening was the capture of President Davis near Irwinville, in southern Georgia. This occurred May 10, 1865; and the conflict, so vigorously prosecuted against overwhelming odds, was ended.

The rest of the story is soon told. Governor Brown resigned his post June 29, 1865. He had officiated as such for almost four terms. Hon. James Johnson—a presidential appointee,—was installed as his successor. As provisional governor of Georgia, he continued to act for several months. Hon. Charles J. Jenkins superseded him as executive in December, 1865. On the summary removal of the former (Jenkins) in January, 1868, Brigadier-General Thomas H. Ruger, U. S. A., became Chief Magistrate in his stead. He is remembered as the military governor of Georgia, and during his incumbency, Atlanta became the State Capital. On

the inauguration of Rufus B. Bullock, six months later, his short-lived reign terminated. Ruger's displace-
ment, however, did not bring the relief for which the
people craved. Bullock riveted on Georgia more se-
curely than ever, the chains of reconstructed recon-
struction. He did not want the State to be re-admitted. The truth is, compliance with the Fourteenth
and Fifteenth Amendments to the Federal Constitution was the test for re-admission into the Union. Bullock did not recognize the commonwealth's eligibility
for that honor. But Ulysses S. Grant, president of the
United States, thought differently. On the 15th of
July, 1870, he signed a Congressional Bill, which de-
clared that Georgia, having fulfilled all requirements,
was adjudged as legally entitled to re-admission into
the Union.

In October, 1871, Governor Bullock, through resignation, brought his inglorious administration to an
end. Thereupon, Benjamin Conley became his successor. A twelve month later, Democracy was definitely
reinstated through the election of James M. Smith. His
tenure was followed by that of General Alfred H. Colquitt, admiringly referred to as the Christian Chief
Magistrate. Then came the short but able term of Alexander H. Stephens. On his death in the spring of
1883, James S. Boynton assumed the gubernatorial
reins. He was not, however, permitted to retain them,
as Henry D. McDaniel was soon saluted as Georgia's
ruler. In 1886 General John B. Gordon was proudly
installed as governor. His administration was an emi-
nently satisfactory one. About twelve years later, when
W. Y. Atkinson was the incumbent, the Spanish-Ameri-
can War began. The sensation which it created was
slight and short-lived. During all this time, the commonwealth prospered, and there was a healthy development along all lines. In 1907 Hoke Smith was inau-
gurated. His tenure, which, in the judgment of many,

15

has been forceful and capable, is nearing its close. He will soon be superseded by Joseph M. Brown, the son of Georgia's famous War Governor. When Mr. Brown becomes the executive, he will have the honor of presiding over a pivotal Southern State, with a population approximating two million, eight hundred and fifty thousand souls, and a great and splendid future.

GOVERNORS OF GEORGIA.

1. JAMES EDWARD OGLETHORPE, Special Agent of the Trustees in the colonization; de facto civil and military governor of the Province; subsequently appointed General and Commander-in-Chief of His Majesty's Forces in Georgia and South Carolina, 1732-1743.
2. WILLIAM STEPHENS, President of the Colony 1743-1751.
3. HENRY PARKER, President of the Colony 1751-1753.
4. PATRICK GRAHAM, President of the Colony 1753-1754.
5. CAPTAIN JOHN REYNOLDS, First Royal Governor of the Province 1754-1757.
6. HENRY ELLIS, Second Royal Governor of the Province 1757-'60.
7. SIR JAMES WRIGHT, Third Royal Governor of the Province 1760-1782.
8. JAMES HABERSHAM, Acting Royal Governor of the Province in 1771, during the absence of Sir James Wright.
9. WILLIAM EWEN, President of the Council of Safety, and, virtute officii, President of Republican Georgia in 1775.
10. ARCHIBALD BULLOCH, President and Commander-in-Chief of Republican Georgia in 1776.
11. BUTTON GWINNETT, President and Commander-in-Chief of Republican Georgia in 1777.
12. JONATHAN BRYAN, at one time Acting President and Commander-in-Chief of Republican Georgia in 1777.
13. JOHN ADAM TREUTLEN, First Republican Governor of Georgia, 1777.
14. JOHN HOUSTOUN, Republican Governor of Georgia 1778, and again elected Governor of Georgia 1784.
15. JOHN WEREAT, President of the Executive Council and, de facto, Republican Governor of Georgia 1779.
16. GEORGE WALTON, Elected Republican Governor of Georgia, November 1779, and Governor of Georgia 1789.
17. RICHARD HOWLEY, Elected Republican Governor of Georgia January, 1780.

16

18. GEORGE WELLS, President of Council and, de facto, Governor of Georgia during the absence of Governor Howley in attendance on the Continental Congress, 1780.
19. STEPHEN HEARD, President of Council and, de facto, Governor of Georgia in 1780.
20. MYRICK DAVIES, President of Council and, de facto, Governor of Georgia in 1781.
21. NATHAN BROWNSON, Elected Governor of Georgia in August, 1781.
22. JOHN MARTIN, Elected Governor of Georgia in January, 1782.
23. LYMAN HALL, Elected Governor of Georgia in January, 1783.
24. SAMUEL ELBERT, Elected Governor of Georgia, 1785.
25. EDWARD TELFAIR, Elected Governor of Georgia 1786, and Governor of Georgia 1790-1793.
26. GEORGE MATHEWS, elected Governor of Georgia 1787,—and Governor of Georgia 1793-1796.
27. GEORGE HANDLEY, Elected Governor of Georgia in 1788.
28. JARED IRWIN, Governor of Georgia 1796-1797 and again in 1806-1809.
29. JAMES JACKSON, Governor of Georgia 1798-1801. He was elected on a former occasion (1788) to office of Governor, but declined on account of youth and inexperience.
30. DAVID EMANUEL, Governor of Georgia, 1801.
31. JOSIAH TATTNALL, Governor of Georgia, 1801-1802.
32. JOHN MILLEDGE, Governor of Georgia, 1802-1806.
33. DAVID B. MITCHELL, Governor of Georgia 1809-1813 and again in 1815-1817.
34. PETER EARLY, Governor of Georgia, 1813-1815.
35. WILLIAM RABUN, Governor of Georgia, 1817-1818.
36. MATTHEW TALBOT, Governor of Georgia, 1818-1819.
37. JOHN CLARKE, Governor of Georgia, 1819-1823.
38. GEORGE M. TROUP, Governor of Georgia, 1823-1827.
39. JOHN FORSYTH, Governor of Georgia, 1827-1829.
40. GEORGE R. GILMER, Governor of Georgia 1829-1831 and again 1837-1839.
41. WILSON LUMPKIN, Governor of Georgia, 1831-1835.
42. WILLIAM SCHLEY, Governor of Georgia, 1835-1837.
43. CHARLES J. MCDONALD, Governor of Georgia, 1839-1843.
44. GEORGE W. CRAWFORD, Governor of Georgia, 1843-1847.
45. GEORGE W. TOWNS, Governor of Georgia, 1847-1851.
46. HOWELL COBB, Governor of Georgia, 1851-1853.
47. HERSCHEL V. JOHNSON, Governor of Georgia, 1853-1857.
48. JOSEPH E. BROWN, Governor of Georgia, 1857-1865.

49. JAMES JOHNSON, Provisional Governor of Georgia, in 1865.
50. CHARLES J. JENKINS, Governor of Georgia, 1865-1868.
51. THOMAS H. RUGER, Military Governor of Georgia, in 1868.
52. RUFUS B. BULLOCK, Governor of Georgia, 1868-1871.
53. BENJAMIN CONLEY, Governor of Georgia, 1871-1872.
54. JAMES M. SMITH, Governor of Georgia, 1872-1876.
55. ALFRED H. COLQUITT, Governor of Georgia, 1876-1882.
56. ALEXANDER H. STEPHENS, Governor of Georgia, 1882-1883.
57. JAMES S. BOYNTON, Governor of Georgia, 1883.
58. HENRY D. McDANIEL, Governor of Georgia, 1883-1886.
59. JOHN B. GORDON, Governor of Georgia, 1886-1890.
60. WILLIAM J. NORTHEN, Governor of Georgia, 1890-1894.
61. W. Y. ATKINSON, Governor of Georgia, 1894-1898.
62. ALLEN D. CANDLER, Governor of Georgia, 1898-1902.
63. JOSEPH M. TERRELL, Governor of Georgia, 1902-1907.
64. HOKE SMITH, Governor of Georgia, 1907-1909.
65. JOSEPH M. BROWN, Goverrnor of Georgia, 1909—.

COUNTIES OF GEORGIA AND DATES OF THEIR FOUNDING.

APPLING, founded in December, 1818.
BAKER, founded in December, 1825.
BALDWIN, founded in May, 1803. ˙
BANKS, founded in December, 1858.
BARTOW, founded in December, 1861.
BEN HILL, founded in July, 1906.
BERRIEN, founded in February, 1856.
BIBB, founded in December, 1822.
BROOKS, founded in December, 1858.
BRYAN, founded in December, 1793.
BULLOCH, founded in February, 1796.
BURKE, founded in 1777.
BUTTS, founded in December, 1825.

CALHOUN, founded in February, 1854.
CAMDEN, founded in 1777.
CAMPBELL, founded in December, 1828.
CARROLL, founded in December, 1826.
CATOOSA, founded in December, 1853.
CHARLTON, founded in February, 1854.
CHATHAM, founded in 1777. ˈ
CHATTAHOOCHEE, founded in February, 1854.
CHATTOOGA, founded in December, 1838.
CHEROKEE, founded in December, 1831.
CLARKE, founded in December, 1801.
CLAY, founded in February, 1854.
CLAYTON, founded in November, 1858.
CLINCH, founded in February, 1850.
COBB, founded in December, 1832.
COFFEE, founded in February, 1854.
COLQUITT, founded in February, 1856.
COLUMBIA, founded in December, 1790.
COWETA, founded in December, 1826.
CRAWFORD, founded in December, 1822.
CRISP, founded in August, 1905.

DADE, founded in December, 1837.
DAWSON, founded in December, 1857.

DECATUR, founded in December, 1823.
DEKALB, founded in December, 1822.
DODGE, founded in October, 1870.
DOOLY, founded in May, 1821.
DOUGHERTY, founded in December, 1853.
DOUGLAS, founded in October, 1870.

EARLY, founded in December, 1818.
ECHOLS, founded in December, 1858.
EFFINGHAM, founded in 1777.
ELBERT, founded in December, 1790.
EMANUEL, founded in December, 1812.

FANNIN, founded in January, 1854.
FAYETTE, founded in May, 1821.
FLOYD, founded December, 1832.
FORSYTH, founded December, 1832.
FRANKLIN, founded February, 1784.
FULTON, founded December, 1853.

GILMER, founded December, 1832.
GLASCOCK, founded December, 1857.
GLYNN, founded 1777.
GORDON, founded Feb. 1850.
GRADY, founded August, 1905.
GREENE, founded February, 1786.
GWINNETT, founded December, 1818.

HABERSHAM, founded December, 1818.
HALL, founded December, 1818.
HANCOCK, founded December, 1793.
HARALSON, founded January, 1856.
HARRIS, founded December, 1827.
HART, founded December, 1853.
HEARD, founded December, 1830.
HENRY, founded May, 1821.
HOUSTOUN, founded May, 1821.

IRWIN, founded December, 1818.

JACKSON, founded February, 1796.
JASPER, founded December, 1812.
JEFF DAVIS, founded August, 1905.
JEFFERSON. founded February, 1796.
JENKINS, founded August, 1905.
JOHNSON, founded December, 1858.
JONES, founded December, 1807.

LAURENS, founded December, 1807.
LEE, founded December, 1826.
LIBERTY, founded 1777.

20

LINCOLN, founded February, 1796.
LOWNDES, founded December, 1825.
LUMPKIN, founded December, 1832.

MCDUFFIE, founded October, 1870.
MCINTOSH, founded December, 1793.
MACON, founded December, 1837.
MADISON, founded December, 1811.
MARION, founded December, 1827.
MERIWETHER, founded December, 1827.
MILLER, founded February, 1856.
MILTON, founded December, 1857.
MITCHELL, founded December, 1857.
MONROE, founded May, 1821.
MONTGOMERY, founded December, 1793.
MORGAN, founded December, 1807.
MURRAY, founded December, 1832.
MUSCOGEE, founded December, 1826.

NEWTON, founded December, 1821.

OCONEE, founded February, 1875.
OGLETHORPE, founded December, 1793.

PAULDING, founded December, 1832.
PICKENS, founded December, 1853.
PIERCE, founded December, 1857.
PIKE, founded December, 1822.
POLK, founded December, 1851.
PULASKI, founded December, 1808.
PUTNAM, founded December, 1807.

QUITMAN, founded December, 1858.

RABUN, founded December, 1819.
RANDOLPH, founded December, 1828
RICHMOND, founded 1777.
ROCKDALE, founded October, 1870.

SCHLEY, founded December, 1857.
SCREVEN, founded December, 1793.
SPALDING, founded December, 1851.
STEWART, founded December, 1830.
STEPHENS, founded August, 1905.
SUMTER, founded December, 1831.

TALBOT, founded December, 1827.
TALIAFERRO, founded December, 1825.
TATTNALL, founded December, 1801.
TAYLOR, founded January, 1852.
TELFAIR, founded December, 1807.
TERRELL, founded February, 1856.

THOMAS, founded December, 1825.
TIFT, founded August, 1905.
TOOMBS, founded August, 1905.
TOWNS, founded March, 1856.
TROUP, founded December, 1826.
TURNER, founded August, 1905.
TWIGGS, founded in December, 1809.

UNION, founded December, 1832.
UPSON, founded December, 1824.

WALKER, founded December, 1833.
WALTON, founded December, 1818.
WARE, founded December, 1824.
WARREN, founded December, 1793.
WASHINGTON, founded February, 1784.
WAYNE, founded May, 1803.
WEBSTER, founded February, 1856.
WHITE, founded December, 1857.
WHITEFIELD, founded December, 1851.
WILCOX, founded December, 1857.
WILKES, founded 1777.
WILKINSON, founded May, 1803.
WORTH, founded December, 1853.

FIELD OFFICERS, REGIMENTS AND BATTALIONS FROM GEORGIA IN THE CONFEDERATE STATES ARMY.

Infantry.

FIRST INFANTRY REGIMENT (1st Georgia Regulars Infantry.)
Chastain, E. W., lieutenant-colonel.
Grieve, Miller, Jr., major, lieutenant-colonel.
Harden, E. R., major.
Hill, A. A. Franklin, major.
Magill, William J., lieutenant-colonel, colonel.
Martin, William, lieutenant-colonel.
Smith, William D., major.
Walker, John D., major.
Wayne, Richard A., major, lieutenant-colonel, colonel.
Williams, Charles J., colonel.
NOTE.—Among the gallant field officers of First Georgia Regulars, Infantry, were Captain John Milledge, of Company D, and Captain J. G. Montgomery, of Company G.

SECOND INFANTRY REGIMENT.
Butt, Edgar M., major, colonel.
Charlton, William W., major.
Harris, Skidmore, lieutenant-colonel.
Harris, William T., major, lieutenant-colonel.
Holmes, William R., lieutenant-colonel.
Lewis, Abner McC., major.
Semmes, Paul J., colonel.
Shepherd, William S., major, lieutenant-colonel.

THIRD INFANTRY REGIMENT.
Hayes, George E., major.
Jones, John F., major.
Lee, Augustus H., major.
Montgomery, Alex. B., major, lieutenant-colonel, colonel.
NOTE.—It has been, unofficially, stated that, before the end of the War, he was promoted to grade of brigadier-general, P. A. C. S. In justice to him, however, it should be said that he has never claimed specified rank.

Nisbet, Reuben B., lieutenant-colonel.
Reid, James S., lieutenant-colonel.

Snead, Claiborne, lieutenant-colonel.
Sturges, John R., major.
Walker, Edward J., colonel.
Wright, Ambrose R., colonel.

FOURTH INFANTRY REGIMENT.

Cook, Philip, lieutenant-colonel, colonel.
DeGraffenried, Francis H., major.
Doles, George, colonel.
Jordan, William F., major, lieutenant-colonel.
Matthews, John J., lieutenant-colonel.
Nash, Edwin A., major, lieutenant-colonel.
Smith, Robert S., major.
Whitehead, Charles L., major.
Willis, William H., major, lieutenant-colonel, colonel.
Winn, David R. E., major, lieutenant-colonel.

FIFTH INFANTRY REGIMENT.

Ansley, David H., major.
Beall, Thomas, lieutenant-colonel.
Black, William T., colonel.
Daniel, Charles P., major, colonel.
Day, Charles B., lieutenant-colonel.
Hundley, William B., major.
Iverson, John F., lieutenant-colonel.
Jackson, John K., colonel.
Kiddoo, John F., major.
Mangham, Samuel W., colonel.
Salisbury, William L., major.

SIXTH INFANTRY REGIMENT.

Anderson, Charles D., major, lieutenant-colonel.
Arnold, William M., major, lieutenant-colonel.
Cleveland, Wilde C., major, lieutenant-colonel.
Colquitt, Alfred H., colonel.
Culpepper, James M., major.
Harris, Sampson W., lieutenant-colonel.
Lofton, John T., lieutenant-colonel, colonel.
Newton, James M., lieutenant-colonel.
Tracy, Phil, major.

SEVENTH INFANTRY REGIMENT.

Almon, Moses T., major, lieutenant-colonel.
Anderson, Lemuel B., major.
Carmichael (Carmical?), George H., major, lieutenant-colonel, colonel.
Cooper, James F., lieutenant-colonel.
Dunwody, John, major, lieutenant-colonel.
Gartrell, Lucius J., colonel.
Hoyle, E. W., major.

Kiser, John F., major.
White, William W., lieutenant-colonel, colonel.
Wilson, William T., colonel.
Witt, Horace H., major.
EIGHTH INFANTRY REGIMENT.
Bartow, F. S., colonel.
Cooper, John F., major.
Cooper, Thomas L., major, lieutenant-colonel.
Dawson, George O., major.
Gardner, William M., lieutenant-colonel, colonel.
Lamar, L. M., major, lieutenant-colonel, colonel.
Magruder, Edward J., major, lieutenant-colonel.
Towers, John R., lieutenant-colonel, colonel.
NINTH INFANTRY REGIMENT.
Arnold, John W., major.
Beck, Benjamin, colonel.
Goulding, E. R., colonel.
Hoge, Edward F., lieutenant-colonel, colonel.
Jones, William M., major.
Mounger, John C. L., Sr., major, lieutenant-colonel.
Turnipseed, Richard A., lieutenant-colonel, colonel.
Webb, John G., major, lieutenant-colonel.
TENTH INFANTRY REGIMENT.
Cumming, Alfred, lieutenant-colonel, colonel.
Hawes, Richard R., major.
Holt, Willis C., major, lieutenant-colonel, colonel.
Kibbee, Charles C., lieutenant-colonel.
Loud, Philologus H., major.
McBride, Andrew J., colonel.
McLaws, LaFayette, colonel.
Weems, John B., major, lieutenant-colonel, colonel
ELEVENTH INFANTRY REGIMENT.
Anderson, George T., colonel.
Goode, Charles T., major.
Guerry, Theodore L., lieutenant-colonel.
Little, Francis H., colonel.
Luffman, William, major, lieutenant-colonel.
McDaniel, Henry D., major.
Welsh, Western R., major.
TWELFTH INFANTRY REGIMENT.
Blandford, Mark H., lieutenant-colonel.
Carson, John T., major.
Conner, Z. T., lieutenant-colonel, colonel.
Hardeman, Isaac, major, lieutenant-colonel.
Hawkins, Willis A., major, lieutenant-colonel.
Johnson, Edward, colonel.

Scott, Thaddeus B., lieutenant-colonel.
Smead, Abner, major, lieutenant-colonel.
Willis, Edward, major, lieutenant-colonel, colonel.

Thirteenth Infantry Regiment.
Baker, John H., major, lieutenant-colonel, colonel.
Douglass, Marcellus, lieutenant-colonel, colonel.
Ector, Walton, colonel.
Jones, S. W., lieutenant-colonel.
Maltbie, Richard, major, lieutenant-colonel.
Moore, John L., major.
Smith, James M., major, lieutenant-colonel, colonel.

Fourteenth Infantry Regiment.
Brumby, A. V., colonel.
Fielder, James M., major, lieutenant-colonel.
Folsom, Robert W., lieutenant-colonel, colonel.
Goldsmith, Washington L., major, lieutenant-colonel.
Harris, William A., major, lieutenant-colonel.
Kelley, Charles C., major.
Lester, Richard P., major, lieutenant-colonel, colonel.
Price, Felix, colonel.
Ramsay, Whiteford S., lieutenant-colonel.

Fifteenth Infantry Regiment.
DuBose, Dudley M., colonel.
Hearnsberger, Stephen Z., lieutenant-colonel.
McIntosh, William M., major, lieutenant-colonel, colonel.
Millican, William T., lieutenant-colonel, colonel.
Shannon, Peter J., major, lieutenant-colonel.
Smith, Joseph T., major.
Smith, Theophilus J., major, lieutenant-colonel.
Stephens, Linton, lieutenant-colonel.
Thomas, Thomas W., colonel.

Sixteenth Infantry Regiment (Sallie Twiggs Regiment.)
Bryan, Goode, lieutenant-colonel, colonel.
Cobb, Howell, colonel.
Gholston, James S., major, lieutenant-colonel, colonel.
Skelton, John H., major.
Stiles, B. Edward, lieutenant-colonel.
Thomas, Henry P., major, lieutenant-colonel, colonel.

Seventeenth Infantry Regiment.
Barden, William A., major, lieutenant-colonel.
Benning, Henry L., colonel.
Hodges, Wesley C., lieutenant-colonel, colonel.
Matthews, Charles W., lieutenant-colonel.
Moore, James B., major.
Pickett, John H., major.
Walker, Thomas, major.

EIGHTEENTH INFANTRY REGIMENT.
Armstrong, Joseph, colonel.
Calahan, W. G., major.
Ford, Francis M., lieutenant-colonel.
Griffis, John C., major.
Johnson, Jefferson, major.
Ruff, S. Z., lieutenant-colonel, colonel.
Stewart, Joseph A., major.
Wofford, William T., colonel.
NINETEENTH INFANTRY REGIMENT.
Boyd, William W., colonel.
Flynt, Tilman W., lieutenant-colonel.
Hamilton, William, major.
Hogan, Ridgeway B., lieutenant-colonel.
Hooper, John W., major.
Hutchins, Andrew J., major, lieutenant-colonel, colonel.
Johnson, Thomas C., lieutenant-colonel.
Mabry, Charles W., major.
Neal, James H., major, lieutenant-colonel, colonel.
TWENTIETH INFANTRY REGIMENT.
Craig, William, major.
Coffee, John A., major.
Cumming, John B., lieutenant-colonel, colonel.
Gamble, Roger L., major.
Jones, John A., major, lieutenant-colonel, colonel.
Ross, Albert B., major.
Seago, Eli M., lieutenant-colonel.
Smith, William Duncan, colonel.
Waddell, James D., major, colonel.
TWENTY-FIRST INFANTRY REGIMENT.
Glover, Thomas C., major, lieutenant-colonel.
Hooper, Thomas W., major, lieutenant-colonel, colonel.
Lynch, Michael, major.
Mercer, John T., colonel.
Morrison, James J., lieutenant-colonel.
TWENTY-SECOND INFANTRY REGIMENT.
Jones, Robert H., colonel.
Jones, George H., colonel.
Lallerstedt, Lawrence D., major.
McCurry, B. C., lieutenant-colonel.
Pritchett, J. W., lieutenant-colonel.
Wasden, Joseph, major, lieutenant-colonel, colonel.
TWENTY-THIRD INFANTRY REGIMENT.
Ballenger, Marcus R., major, lieutenant-colonel, colonel.
Barclay, William P., lieutenant-colonel, colonel.
Best, Emory F., major, lieutenant-colonel, colonel.

27

Boston, William J., major.
Huggins, James H., major, lieutenant-colonel, colonel.
Hutcherson, Thomas, colonel.
Sharp, John J. A., major, lieutenant-colonel.

TWENTY-FOURTH INFANTRY REGIMENT.
Chandler, Joseph N., lieutenant-colonel.
McMillan, Robert, colonel.
McMillan, Robert E., major.
Sanders, C. C., lieutenant-colonel, colonel.
Smith, Frederick C., major.
Winn, Thomas E., major, lieutenant-colonel.

TWENTY-FIFTH INFANTRY REGIMENT.
Ashley, W. P. M., lieutenant-colonel.
Smith, Albert W., major.
Wilson, Claudius C., colonel.
Williams, Andrew J,. lieutenant-colonel.
Winn, William J., major, colonel.
Wylly, William Henry, major, lieutenant-colonel.

TWENTY-SIXTH (Lamar's) INFANTRY REGIMENT. (Afterward known as 7th Infantry Battalion, which was merged into 61st Infantry.)
Lamar, Charles A. L., colonel.
Lamar, John H., major.
McDonald, James, lieutenant-colonel.

TWENTY-SIXTH (Styles') INFANTRY REGIMENT. (Also called 13th).
Atkinson, Edmund N., colonel.
Blain, James S., major, lieutenant-colonel.
Gardner, Thomas N., major.
Griffin, Eli S., major, lieutenant-colonel.
Grace, Benjamin F., major.
Lane, William A., lieutenant-colonel.
McDonald, William A., lieutenant-colonel.
Styles, Carey W., colonel.

TWENTY-SEVENTH INFANTRY REGIMENT.
Brewer, Septimus L., lieutenant-colonel.
Bussey, Hezekiah, major, lieutenant-colonel.
Dennis, Charles J., major.
Dorsey, Jasper N., lieutenant-colonel.
Gardner, James, major, lieutenant-colonel.
Holliday, Henry B., major.
Rentfro, William H., major, lieutenant-colonel.
Smith, Levi B., colonel.
Stubbs, John W., major, lieutenant-colonel.
Zachry, Charles T., major, lieutenant-colonel, colonel.

28

TWENTY-EIGHTH INFANTRY REGIMENT.
Banning, James W., major.
Cain, James G., major, lieutenant-colonel.
Crawford, William P., lieutenant-colonel.
Graybill, Tully, major, colonel.
Hall, George A., lieutenant-colonel.
Warthen, T. J., colonel.
TWENTY-NINTH INFANTRY REGIMENT.
Alexander, T. W., lieutenant-colonel.
Billopp, W. W., major, lieutenant-colonel.
Knight, Levi J., major.
Lamb, John C., major.
Mitchell, William D., lieutenant-colonel, colonel.
Owen, John J., major.
Spaulding, R., colonel.
Young, William J., colonel.
THIRTIETH INFANTRY REGIMENT.
Bailey, David J., colonel.
Boynton, James S., major, lieutenant-colonel, colonel.
Hendrick, Henry, major.
Mangham, Thomas W., lieutenant-colonel, colonel.
Thorpe, Cicero A., major.
Tidwell, Miles M., lieutenant-colonel.
THIRTY-FIRST INFANTRY REGIMENT. (Also called 27th.)
Crowder, John T., lieutenant-colonel.
Evans, Clement A., major, colonel.
Hill, Daniel P., lieutenant-colonel.
Lowe, John H., major, lieutenant-colonel, colonel.
Phillips, Pleasant J., colonel.
Pride, Rodolphus T., major, lieutenant-colonel.
THIRTY-SECOND INFANTRY REGIMENT.
Bacon, E. H., Jr., major, lieutenant-colonel.
Harrison, George P., Jr., colonel.
Holland, W. T., major.
Pruden, William H., lieutenant-colonel.
THIRTY-THIRD INFANTRY REGIMENT. (Not organized.)
Littlefield, A., colonel.
THIRTY-FOURTH INFANTRY REGIMENT.
Bradley, J. W., lieutenant-colonel.
Dorough, Thomas T., major.
Johnson, J. A. W., colonel.
Jackson, John M., major.
THIRTY-FIFTH INFANTRY REGIMENT.
Bull, Gustavus A., lieutenant-colonel.
Groves, William L., major.

Holt, Bolling H., major, lieutenant-colonel, colonel.
McCullochs, William H., major, lieutenant-colonel.
McElvany, James T., major.
Thomas, Edward L., colonel.
Williams, Lee A. J., major.

THIRTY-SIXTH (Villepigue's) INFANTRY REGIMENT. (Formerly 1st Infantry battalion; afterward 1st Confederate. Was also called Georgia and Mississippi Regiment of Infantry.)
Lovell, William S., major.
Smith, George A., lieutenant-colonel.
Villepigue, John B., colonel.

THIRTY-SIXTH (Glenn's) INFANTRY REGIMENT.
Broyles, Charles E., major, colonel.
Glenn, Jesse A., colonel.
Loudermilk, John, major.
Wallace, Alexander M., lieutenant-colonel.

THIRTY-SEVENTH INFANTRY REGIMENT. (3d and 4th Battalions Infantry consolidated.)
Bradford, Jesse J., major.
Kendrick, Meredith, major.
Rudler, Anthony F., colonel.
Smith, Joseph T., lieutenant-colonel.
Wilson, Robert E., major.

THIRTY-SEVENTH (Military District) GEORGIA REGIMENT.
Cato, William W., lieutenant-colonel.

THIRTY-EIGHTH INFANTRY REGIMENT. (Wright's Legion.)
Bomar, Thomas H., major.
Davant, Phillip E., lieutenant-colonel.
Flowers, John Y., major.
Lee, George W., lieutenant-colonel, colonel.
Mathews, James D., major, lieutenant-colonel, colonel.
Parr, Lewis J., major, lieutenant-colonel.
Wright, Augustus R., colonel.

THIRTY-NINTH INFANTRY REGIMENT.
Jackson, J. F. B., lieutenant-colonel.
McConnell, J. T., colonel.
Milton, William P., lieutenant-colonel.
Pitner, Tilmon H., major.
Randell, Gabriel H., major.

FORTIETH INFANTRY REGIMENT.
Camp, Raleigh S., major.
Johnson, Abda, colonel.
Young, Robert M., lieutenant-colonel.

FORTY-FIRST INFANTRY REGIMENT.
Curtis, William E., lieutenant-colonel, colonel.

Knight, John, major.
McDaniel, Charles A., colonel.
Nall, Mark S., major.

FORTY-SECOND INFANTRY REGIMENT.
Henderson, Robert J., colonel.
Hulsey, William H., major, lieutenant-colonel.
Maddox, Robert F,. lieutenant-colonel.
Thomas, Lovick P., major.

FORTY-THIRD INFANTRY REGIMENT.
Bell, Hiram P., lieutenant-colonel, colonel.
Harris, Skidmore, colonel.
Kellogg, Henry C., major, lieutenant-colonel, colonel.
Lester, William C., major.

FORTY-FOURTH INFANTRY REGIMENT.
Adams, Joseph W., major.
Banks, Richard O., major.
Beck, James W., major, lieutenant-colonel.
Estes, John B., lieutenant-colonel, colonel.
Key, John C., major.
Lumpkin, Samuel P., lieutenant-colonel, colonel.
Peebles, William H., major, lieutenant-colonel, colonel.
Smith, Robert A., colonel.

FORTY-FIFTH INFANTRY REGIMENT.
Carter, James W., major, lieutenant-colonel.
Conn, Charles A., major, lieutenant-colonel.
Gibson, Aurelius W., major.
Grice, Washington L., major, lieutenant-colonel.
Hardeman, Thomas, Jr., colonel.
Rogers, Matthew R., major.
Simmons, Thomas J., lieutenant-colonel, colonel.
Wallace, William S., major, lieutenant-colonel.

FORTY-SIXTH INFANTRY REGIMENT.
Colquitt, Peyton H., colonel.
Daniel, William A., lieutenant-colonel.
Dunlop, Samuel J. C., major, colonel.
Speer, Alexander M., major.

FORTY-SEVENTH INFANTRY REGIMENT.
Cone, James G., major.
Cone, Joseph S., major, lieutenant-colonel.
Edwards, A. C., lieutenant-colonel, colonel.
Phillips, William S., lieutenant-colonel.
Williams, G. W. M., colonel.

FORTY-EIGHTH INFANTRY REGIMENT.
Carswell, Reuben W., lieutenant-colonel.
Gibson, William, colonel.

Hall, Matthew R., major, lieutenant-colonel, colonel.
Whitehead, John R., major.

Forty-ninth Infantry Regiment.

Cooke, Oliver H., lieutenant-colonel.
Duggan, James B., major.
Durham, John A., major.
Jordan, John T., lieutenant-colonel, colonel.
Lane, A. J., colonel.
Manning, Seaborn M., lieutenant-colonel.
Pate, John H., major.
Player, Samuel T., major, lieutenant-colonel, colonel.
Rivers, Jonathan, major, lieutenant-colonel.
Williams, Wiley J., major, lieutenant-colonel.

Fiftieth Infantry Regiment.

Curry, Duncan, major.
Fleming, William O., major, lieutenant-colonel.
Kearse, Francis, lieutenant-colonel.
Manning, William R., colonel.
McGlashan, Peter A. S., colonel.

NOTE.—We learn, unofficially, that, had not the War ended, his commission as brigadier-general, P. A. C. S., might, in all likelihood, have reached him. He was a gallant soldier.

Pendleton, P. C., major.
Sheffield, Pliny, major, lieutenant-colonel.
Spence, John M., major.

Fifty-first Infantry Regiment.

Anthony, Oliver P., major, lieutenant-colonel.
Ball, Edward, lieutenant-colonel, colonel.
Crawford, John P., major, lieutenant-colonel.
Dickey, James, major, lieutenant-colonel, colonel.
Dunwody, Henry M., major.
Slaughter, W. M., colonel.

Fifty-second Infantry Regiment.

Boyd, Wier, colonel.
Findley, J. J., major.
Moore, John J., major.
Phillips, Charles D., lieutenant-colonel, colonel.
Van Diviere, Solomon H., lieutenant-colonel.

Fifty-third Infantry Regiment.

Brown, Sheridan R., major.
Doyal, Leonard T., colonel.
Hance, J. W., lieutenant-colonel.
Hartsfield, W. F., major, lieutenant-colonel.
Simms, James P., major, colonel.
Sims, Thomas W., major.

Sloan, Thomas, lieutenant-colonel.
Taylor, Robert P., lieutenant-colonel.
FIFTY-FOURTH INFANTRY REGIMENT.
Mann, William H., major.
Rawls, Morgan, lieutenant-colonel.
Way, Charlton H., colonel.
FIFTY-FIFTH INFANTRY REGIMENT.
Harkie, C. B., colonel.
Persons, A. W., lieutenant-colonel, colonel.
Printup, Daniel S., major.
FIFTY-SIXTH INFANTRY REGIMENT.
Brewster, James P., major.
Pool, M. L., major.
Slaughter, J. T., lieutenant-colonel.
Watkins, E. P., colonel.
FIFTY-SEVENTH INFANTRY REGIMENT. (Also called 54th. For-
merly 2d Regiment Georgia State Troops.)
Barkuloo, William, colonel.
Guyton, Cincinnatus S., lieutenant-colonel.
Shinholser, John W., major.
FIFTY-EIGHTH INFANTRY REGIMENT.
(No record.)
FIFTY-NINTH INFANTRY REGIMENT.
Bass, Mastin G., major.
Brown, Jack, colonel.
Fickling, William H., major.
Gee, Bolivar H., major, lieutenant-colonel.
Harris, Charles J., major, lieutenant-colonel.
Hunter, George R., lieutenant-colonel.
SIXTIETH INFANTRY REGIMENT. (Formed from Stiles' 4th Bat-
talion.)
Berry, Thomas J., lieutenant-colonel.
Jones, Waters B., major, colonel.
Stiles, William H., Sr., colonel.
SIXTY-FIRST INFANTRY REGIMENT. (Also called 26th.)
Brenan, Peter, major.
Lamar, John Hill, colonel.
McArthur, Charles W., major, lieutenant-colonel.
McDuffie, James Y., lieutenant-colonel.
MacRae, Archibald P., major.
Tillman, Henry, major.
VanValkenburg, James D., major.
SIXTY-SECOND REGIMENT PARTISAN RANGERS. (See Cavalry.)
SIXTY-THIRD INFANTRY REGIMENT. Formed from 13th Infan-
try Battalion.)
Allen, Joseph V. H., major.

Black, George R., lieutenant-colonel.
Giles, John R., major.
Gordon, George A., colonel.

SIXTY-FOURTH INFANTRY REGIMENT.
Barrow, James, lieutenant-colonel.
Evans, John W., colonel.
Jenkins, Charles S., major, lieutenant-colonel.
Thomas, George S., major.
Weems, Walter H., major, lieutenant-colonel, colonel.

SIXTY-FIFTH INFANTRY REGIMENT. (Formed from Infantry
Battalion of Smith's Legion.)
Fain, John S., lieutenant-colonel, colonel.
Foster, William G., colonel.
Moore, Robert H., lieutenant-colonel, colonel.
Pearcy, Jacob W., major, lieutenant-colonel.
Smith, Sumner J., colonel.
Williams, Samuel F., major.

SIXTY-SIXTH INFANTRY REGIMENT. (Also called 65th Regiment.)
Andrews, John F., major (declined appointment).
Hamilton, A. S., lieutenant-colonel.
Hull, R. Newton, major.
Nisbet, J. Cooper, colonel.

FIRST INFANTRY BATTALION. (Merged into 36th (Villepigue's)
Georgia, afterward 1st Confederate.)
Larey, Peter H., major.
Lovell, William S., major.
Villepigue, John B., major, lieutenant-colonel.

SECOND INDEPENDENT INFANTRY BATTALION.
Hardeman, Thomas, Jr., major.
Moffett, Charles W., major.
Ross, George W., major.

THIRD INFANTRY BATTALION. (United with 17th Battalion.
formed the 37th Georgia.)
Rudler, Anthony F., major, lieutenant-colonel.
Stovall, Marcellus A., lieutenant-colonel.

FOURTH (Mercer's) INFANTRY BATTALION. (Merged into 21st
Infantry.)
Mercer, John T., lieutenant-colonel.
Morrison, James J., major.

FOURTH (Stiles') INFANTRY BATTALION. (Merged into 60th
Georgia.)
Berry, Thomas J., major.
Stiles, William H., Sr., lieutenant-colonel.

SEVENTH INFANTRY BATTALION. (Formerly Lamar's 26th Infantry. Merged into 61st Georgia.)

34

Lamar, Charles A. L., lieutenant-colonel.
Lamar, John H., major, lieutenant-colonel.
EIGHTH INFANTRY BATTALION.
Gray, John W., major.
Hunt, B. F., major.
Littlefield, Asahel, lieutenant-colonel.
Morgan, Edward F., major.
Napier, Leroy, Jr., lieutenant-colonel.
Reid, J. T., lieutenant-colonel.
Watters, Zachariah L., major, lieutenant-colonel.
NINTH INFANTRY BATTALION. (Also called 17th Battalion.)
Smith, Joseph T., major.
TENTH INFANTRY BATTALION. (Also called 3d Battalion.)
Frederick, James D., major.
Rylander, John E., major.
THIRTEENTH INFANTRY BATTALION. (Merged into 63d Regiment.)
Gordon, George A., major.
SEVENTEENTH INFANTRY BATTALION. (See 9th Battalion.)
EIGHTEENTH INFANTRY BATTALION. (Savannah Volunteer Guards.)
Basinger, William S., major.
Screven, John, major.
TWENTY-SIXTH INFANTRY BATTALION.
Nisbet, John W., major.
TWENTY-SEVENTH INFANTRY BATTALION.
Hartridge, Alfred L., major.
Stubbs, William B., major.
FIRST BATTALION SHARPSHOOTERS. (Note—Capt. Richard Cuyler King, as the senior officer present, was in command of this Battalion at the time of his capture at the Battle of Nashville, December 16, 1864. He had held the position for several months.)
Anderson, Robert H., major.
Shaaff, Arthur, major.
FIRST INFANTRY BATTALION GEORGIA RESERVES.
Symons, William R., major.
FIRST GEORGIA VOLUNTEERS INFANTRY. (Disbanded.)
Anderson, James W., major.
Ramsey, James N., colonel.
Thompson, George H., lieutenant-colonel.
FIRST VOLUNTEERS GEORGIA INFANTRY.
Ford, Martin J., major, lieutenant-colonel.
Mercer, Hugh W., colonel.
Olmstead, Charles H., major, colonel.
Rockwell, William S., lieutenant-colonel.

First Regiment Infantry Georgia State Guard.
Dabney, William H., colonel.
Groves, John F., major.
Jones, Richard W., lieutenant-colonel.
First Regiment Georgia State Troops.
Brown, ——, lieutenant-colonel.
Galt, E. M., colonel.
Tate, William, major.
First Regiment Local Defense Troops, Macon, Georgia.
Brooks, T., lieutenant-colonel.
First (Fannin's) Regiment Georgia Reserves.
Fannin, James H., colonel.
Neely, James J., lieutenant-colonel.
Park, John W., mayor.
First (Symons') Regiment Georgia Reserves.
Cunningham, John, major.
Symons, William R., colonel.
First City Battalion, Columbus, Georgia. (Detailed Men.)
Jaques, Samuel R., major.
First Division Georgia Militia.
Flournoy, R. W., colonel.
First Georgia Light Duty Men, Macon, Ga.
Rowland, Alexander M., major.
First Regiment Local Defense Troops, Augusta, Ga. (Note—
Rains, George W., colonel. Commissioned as major
of artillery, P. A. C. S., July 10, 1861; he was then
specially detailed to supervise the erection of the
Augusta (Ga.) Powder Works. His highest com-
missioned rank was that of colonel. Died at New-
burgh, N. Y., March 21, 1898.)
Moore, John C., lieutenant-colonel.
Second Battalion Sharpshooters.
Cox, J. J., major.
Whiteley, Richard H., major.
Second Regiment Georgia Reserves.
Jones, C. M., lieutenant-colonel.
Maddox, Robert F., colonel.
Powell, W. A., major.
Second Regiment Georgia State Line.
Wilson, James, colonel.
Second (Storey's) Regiment Georgia State Troops.
Storey, R. L., colonel.
Second (Stapleton's) Regiment Georgia State Troops.
Stapleton, ——, colonel.
Second Battalion Local Defense Troops, Macon, Ga.
Walker, E. W., major, (acting).

SECOND DIVISION GEORGIA MILITIA.
Armstrong, ——, colonel.
THIRD BATTALION SHARPSHOOTERS.
Davant, Philip E., major.
Hutchins, Nathan L., Jr., lieutenant-colonel.
Simmons, William E., major.
Smith, H. H., major.
THIRD REGIMENT, GEORGIA RESERVES.
Griffin, J. B., major.
Harris, Charles J., colonel.
Moore, J. L., lieutenant-colonel.
THIRD REGIMENT, FIRST BRIGADE, GEORGIA STATE TROOPS.
Johnson, ——, colonel.
FOURTH BATTALION SHARPSHOOTERS. (Formed from part of 3d
Inf. Battalion.)
Caswell, Theodore D., major.
FOURTH BATTALION GEORGIA STATE GUARD.
Whitehead, Archer, major.
FOURTH REGIMENT GEORGIA RESERVES.
Burks, J. H., major.
Candler, A. D., lieutenant-colonel.
Taylor, Richard S., colonel.
FOURTH REGIMENT, SECOND BRIGADE, GEORGIA STATE TROOPS.
Gant, ——, colonel.
FIRST AUGUSTA BATTALION OF INFANTRY.
Jackson, George T., major.
FIFTH INFANTRY BATTALION, GEORGIA STATE GUARD.
Wilson, William A., major.
FIFTH INFANTRY REGIMENT, GEORGIA STATE GUARD.
Curley, Barnard, major.
Hargett, Flynn, lieutenant-colonel.
Salisbury, William L., colonel.
FIFTH REGIMENT GEORGIA RESERVES.
Cumming, John B., colonel.
Findlay, C. D., lieutenant-colonel.
McGregor, C. E., major.
FIFTH REGIMENT GEORGIA STATE TROOPS.
Mann, ——, colonel.
SIXTH INFANTRY REGIMENT GEORGIA STATE GUARD.
Lofton, William A., major, colonel.
Mangham, Samuel W., lieutenant-colonel.
Nunnally, Aaron D., major.
SIXTH REGIMENT GEORGIA STATE TROOPS.
Thompson, ——, colonel.
SEVENTH INFANTRY REGIMENT GEORGIA STATE GUARD.
Latimer, Reuben, major.

Lester, George N., colonel.
Neely, James J., lieutenant-colonel.
SEVENTH REGIMENT GEORGIA STATE TROOPS.
Redding, A. F., colonel.
EIGHTH INFANTRY REGIMENT GEORGIA STATE GUARD.
Fowler, John W., lieutenant-colonel.
Henderson, John T., colonel.
Pinckard, James S., major.
EIGHTH REGIMENT GEORGIA MILITIA.
Rountree, C. N., colonel.
EIGHTH REGIMENT GEORGIA STATE TROOPS.
Chastain, E. W., colonel.
EIGHTH REGIMENT, THIRD BRIGADE, GEORGIA STATE TROOPS.
Scott, ——, colonel.
NINTH INFANTRY REGIMENT GEORGIA STATE GUARD.
Mell, P. H., colonel.
Peacock, Thomas P., major.
Walker, Dickerson H., lieutenant-colonel.
NINTH REGIMENT, THIRD BRIGADE, GEORGIA STATE TROOPS.
Hill, J. M., colonel.
TENTH REGIMENT GEORGIA STATE TROOPS.
Davis, C. M., colonel.
ELEVENTH INFANTRY BATTALION, GEORGIA STATE GUARD.
Cooper, John, major.
ELEVENTH INFANTRY REGIMENT GEORGIA STATE GUARD.
Godfrey, William, lieutenant-colonel.
McGriff, Patrick A., major.
McIntyre, Archibald T., colonel.
ELEVENTH REGIMENT GEORGIA STATE TROOPS.
Price, J. V., colonel.
THIRTEENTH (Yarborough's) INFANTRY BATTALION GEORGIA
STATE GUARD.
Yarborough, Christopher C., major.
FOURTEENTH INFANTRY BATTALION GEORGIA STATE GUARD (Ma-
con Battalion.)
Jones, John E., major.
SEVENTEENTH BATTALION INFANTRY, GEORGIA STATE GUARD.
McGee, J. W., major.
EIGHTEENTH INFANTRY BATTALION GEORGIA STATE GUARD (Au-
gusta Fire Battalion.)
Day, Charles B., major.
Platt, Charles A., lieutenant-colonel.
NINETEENTH (Thompson's) INFANTRY BATTALION GEORGIA
STATE GUARD. (City Guard Battalion, Columbus,
Ga.)

Bivins, James M., major.

Thompson, Dexter B., lieutenant-colonel.

TWENTIETH (Wright's) INFANTRY BATTALION GEORGIA STATE GUARD. (Merged into 12th Regiment Georgia State Guard.)

Wright, Henry G., major.

TWENTY-FIRST INFANTRY BATTALION GEORGIA STATE GUARD. (Merged into Wright's 12th Regiment.)

Kenedy, James B., major.

TWENTY-SECOND INFANTRY BATTALION GEORGIA STATE GUARD.

Carswell, Nathaniel A., lieutenant-colonel.

Hughes, Daniel G., major.

TWENTY-THIRD INFANTRY BATTALION GEORGIA STATE GUARD.

Cook, F. W. C., major.

THE FIVE GEORGIA INFANTRY LEGIONS.

1. SMITH'S GEORGIA LEGION, commanded by Sumner J. Smith.

2. WRIGHT'S GEORGIA LEGION, commanded by Col. Augustus R. Wright.

3. COBB'S GEORGIA LEGION, commanded by Col. Thos. R. R. Cobb.

4. PHILLIPS' GEORGIA LEGION, commanded by Col. Wm. Phillips.

5. THOMAS' GEORGIA LEGION. The name of commander, or organizer of this Legion, can not be ascertained. It is reported in Avery's History of Georgia that the numerical strength of that Legion was three hundred and ninety-five (395). I can find no mention of this Legion in the Official Records.

CAVALRY.

FIRST CAVALRY REGIMENT.
Davitte, Samuel W., major, lieutenant-colonel, colonel.
Harper, A. R., major, lieutenant-colonel.
Morrison, James J., lieutenant-colonel, colonel.
Strickland, James H., major, lieutenant-colonel.
Tench, John W., major.
Watts, George T., lieutenant-colonel.

SECOND CAVALRY REGIMENT.
Crews, Charles C., colonel.
Dunlop, James E., lieutenant-colonel.
Hood, Arthur, lieutenant-colonel.
Ison, Francis M., major, lieutenant-colonel.
Lawton, William J., colonel.
Mayo, James W., major.
Whaley, C. A., major.

THIRD CAVALRY REGIMENT.
Booton, Daniel F., major.
Crawford, Martin J., colonel.
Johnson, Hiram H., major.
Kennon, Richard E., lieutenant-colonel, colonel.
Thomson, Robert, colonel.
Thornton, James T., lieutenant-colonel.

FOURTH (Avery's) CAVALRY REGIMENT. (Formed from 23d
Avery, Isaac W., colonel.
NOTE.—It has been, unofficially, stated that he was, before the close of the War, promoted to grade of brigadier-general. P. A. C. S. He has, in his History of Georgia, emphasized his belief in fact of his promotion.
Cook, William L., lieutenant-colonel.
Owen, D. Jackson, major.
Stewart, Augustus R., major.

FOURTH (Clinch's) CAVALRY REGIMENT.
Clinch, Duncan L., colonel.
Harris, John L., lieutenant-colonel.
McDonald, Jesse C., major.

FIFTH CAVALRY REGIMENT. (Formed from 1st and 2d Battalions.)
Anderson, Robert H., colonel.
Bird, Edward, lieutenant-colonel, colonel.

Davant, Richard J., Jr., major, lieutenant-colonel.
Wiltberger, William H., major.
SIXTH CAVALRY REGIMENT. (Formed from Cavalry Battalion, Smith's Legion.)
Bale, Alfred F., major.
Brown, B. F., lieutenant-colonel.
Burns, John T., major.
Fain, Joel C., major, lieutenant-colonel.
Hart, John R., colonel.
SEVENTH CAVALRY REGIMENT. (Formed from 21st and 24th Battalions.)
Anderson, Edward C., Jr., major.
NOTE.—He was, we are unofficially informed, successively promoted to grade of lieutenant-colonel and colonel of 7th Cavalry Regiment in 1864; and, had the War continued, might have been advanced to rank of brigadier-general, P. A. C. S. He was a notably gallant soldier.

Davies, John N., major.
McAllister, Joseph L., lieutenant-colonel.
White, William P., colonel.
EIGHTH CAVALRY REGIMENT. (Formed from 62d Regiment and 20th Battalion.)
Griffin, Joel R., colonel.
Millen, John M., lieutenant-colonel.
Thomson, William G., major.
NINTH CAVALRY REGIMENT. (Formed from Cavalry Battalion of Cobb's Legion.)
Jones, Malcolm D., major.
King, Barrington S., lieutenant-colonel.
Wright, Gilbert J., colonel.
TENTH CAVALRY REGIMENT. (Formed from 7th Confederate Cavalry and part of Millen's Georgia Battalion.)
Claiborne, Thomas D., lieutenant-colonel.
Sikes, Jesse H., major.
Taliaferro, V. H., colonel.
ELEVENTH CAVALRY REGIMENT. (Formed from 30th Battalion.)
Barclay, Hugh W., lieutenant-colonel.
Bell, Madison, major.
Young, Andrew, colonel.
TWELFTH CAVALRY REGIMENT. (See Avery's 4th Georgia Cavalry.)
THIRTEENTH CAVALRY REGIMENT. (Formed from 16th Battallion.)
Winn, Samuel J., lieutenant-colonel.
FIRST CAVALRY BATTALION. (Merged into 5th Cavalry.)
Spalding, Charles, lieutenant-colonel.

SECOND CAVALRY BATTALION. (Merged into 5th Georgia Cavalry.)
Bird, Edward, lieutenant-colonel.
Cumming, Montgomery, lieutenant-colonel.
Davant, Richard J., Jr., major.
THIRD CAVALRY BATTALION. (Merged into Clinch's 4th Georgia Cavalry.)
Clinch, Duncan L., major, lieutenant-colonel.
Harris, John L., major.
SIXTEENTH CAVALRY BATTALION. (Merged into 13th Georgia Cavalry.)
Clarke, Edward Y., major.
Nix, F. M., lieutenant-colonel.
Winn, Samuel J., major, lieutenant-colonel.
NINETEENTH CAVALRY BATTALION. (Merged into 10th Confederate Cavalry.)
Goode, Charles T., major.
TWENTY-FIRST CAVALRY BATTALION. (Merged into 7th Georgia Cavalry.) Georgia Partisan Rangers.
White, William P., major.
TWENTY-THIRD CAVALRY BATTALION. (Merged into 4th (Avery's) Georgia Cavalry.)
Avery, Isaac W., lieutenant-colonel.
TWENTY-FOURTH CAVALRY BATTALION. (Merged into 7th Georgia Cavalry.)
Anderson, Edward C., Jr., major.
TWENTY-FIFTH CAVALRY BATTALION. (Provost Battalion, Atlanta, Ga.)
Lee, George W., lieutenant-colonel.
TWENTY-NINTH CAVALRY BATTALION.
Camfield, Charles H., major.
Hood, Arthur, lieutenant-colonel.
THIRTIETH CAVALRY BATTALION. (Merged into 11th Georgia Cavalry.)
Barclay, Hugh W., major.
Young, Andrew, lieutenant-colonel.
FIRST BATTALION CAVALRY MILITIA. (See 16th Battalion Cavalry, Georgia State Guard.)
SECOND CAVALRY REGIMENT, GEORGIA STATE GUARD.
Beasley, W. P., lieutenant-colonel.
Lane, J. M., major.
Willcoxon, John B., colonel.
SECOND REGIMENT, GEORGIA PARTISAN RANGERS.
Hunt, A. A., colonel.

43

THIRD CAVALRY BATTALION, GEORGIA STATE GUARD. (Atlanta Fire Battalion.)
Lee, George W., lieutenant-colonel.
Mecaslin, John H., major.
THIRD CAVALRY REGIMENT, GEORGIA STATE GUARD.
Freeman, John M., major.
Martin, Luther H. O., lieutenant-colonel.
Toombs, Robert, colonel.
FOURTH CAVALRY REGIMENT, GEORGIA STATE GUARD.
Key, P. C., lieutenant-colonel.
Stephens, Samuel, major.
White, Robert, colonel.
SIXTH CAVALRY BATTALION, GEORGIA STATE GUARD.
Culberson, Augustus B., lieutenant-colonel.
Fuller, Haley G., major.
SEVENTH CAVALRY BATTALION, GEORGIA STATE GUARD.
Shivers, James A., major.
Stephens, Linton, lieutenant-colonel.
EIGHTH CAVALRY BATTALION, GEORGIA STATE GUARD.
Stephens, John T., major.
NINTH (McDonald's) CAVALRY BATTALION, GEORGIA STATE GUARD.
Phillips, William, major.
TENTH BATTALION MOUNTED RIFLES, GEORGIA STATE GUARD. (Also called 9th Cavalry Battalion, Georgia State Guard.)
Mell, Pat., lieutenant-colonel.
Price, Hawkins F., major.
TENTH CAVALRY REGIMENT, GEORGIA STATE GUARD.
Floyd, John J., colonel.
Glenn, J. N., lieutenant-colonel.
Hudson, G. L., major.
TWELFTH CAVALRY BATTALION, GEORGIA STATE GUARD.
Stewart, Thomas R., major.
TWELFTH CAVALRY REGIMENT, GEORGIA STATE TROOPS.
Sims, R., colonel.
FIFTEENTH BATTALION, GEORGIA PARTISAN RANGERS. (Merged into 62d Regiment.)
Griffin, Joel R., major, lieutenant-colonel.
FIFTEENTH CAVALRY BATTALION, GEORGIA STATE GUARD.
Jones, E. T., lieutenant-colonel.
SIXTEENTH CAVALRY BATTALION GEORGIA STATE GUARD. (Gilmer Battalion, also called 1st Battalion Georgia Militia.)
West, Doctor M., major.

44

TWENTIETH BATTALION GEORGIA PARTISAN RANGERS. (Part merged into 8th and part into 10th Cavalry.)
  Millen, John M., major, lieutenant-colonel.
  Spencer, Samuel B., major.
  Thomson, William G., major.
SIXTY-SECOND REGIMENT GEORGIA PARTISAN RANGERS. (Formerly 1st Battalion Partisan Rangers; 2d Regiment Partisan Rangers, united with Millen's 20th Battalion, became 8th Cavalry. Part of 62d became 16th Battalion North Carolina Cavalry.)
  Ellis, William L. A., major.
  Griffin, Joel R., colonel.
  Kennedy, John T., major, lieutenant-colonel. (Transferred to 16th Battalion North Carolina Cavalry.)
  Towns, Randolph, lieutenant-colonel.
FIRST CAVALRY BATTALION GEORGIA RESERVES.
  Blount, J. H., colonel.
  Osborn, N. C., major.
  Tufts, Orrin, major.
AUGUSTA ARSENAL BATTALION.
  Girardey, V. J. B., major, (acting).
ATLANTA ARSENAL BATTALION.
  McCall, James K., major.
BRADSHAW'S CAVALRY BATTALION.
  Bradshaw, A. C., major.
CAMDEN COUNTY MILITIA.
  Baily, David, lieutenant-colonel.
  Covedo, John S., major.
  Floyd, Henry H., colonel.
CHEROKEE LEGION, GEORGIA STATE GUARD.
  Grambling, Enoch G., major.
  Hill, Benjamin, lieutenant-colonel.
  Rusk, James E., colonel.
CITY BATTALION, PROVOST GUARD, Columbus, Ga.
  Wilkins, Francis G., major.
COAST GUARD BATTALION, GEORGIA MILITIA.
  Gaulden, William B., colonel.
COBB'S LEGION,—INFANTRY BATTALION.
  Bagley, Ed. F., major.
  Camak, Thomas, major.
  Cobb, Thomas R. R., colonel.
  Conyers, William D., major.
  Garnett, Richard B., lieutenant-colonel.
  Glenn, Luther J., major, lieutenant-colonel.
  Knight, Gazaway B., lieutenant-colonel.

Lamar, Jefferson M., major, lieutenant-colonel.
McDaniel, William W., major.
COBB'S LEGION—CAVALRY BATTALION. (Afterward 9th Cavalry.)
Delony, William G., major, lieutenant-colonel.
King, Barrington S., lieutenant-colonel.
Rice, Zachariah A., major.
Yancey, Benjamin C., major.
Young, Pierce M. B., major, lieutenant-colonel, colonel.
Wright, Gilbert J., major, lieutenant-colonel, colonel.
NOTE.—Among the dashing troopers of this famous Legion, the gallant Captain Francis Edgeworth Eve, of Company K, will long be remembered. He was a born soldier and a sabreur of distinction; and his prowess in battle won him recognition in the Confederate army. Died in 1908.

COOK'S BATTALION. (See 23d Infantry Battalion Georgia State Guard.)
FLOYD LEGION, GEORGIA STATE GUARD.
Alexander, Thomas W., major.
Freeman, John R., lieutenant-colonel.
Yeiser, James G., colonel.
GILMER BATTALION (Cavalry). (See 16th Battalion Georgia State Guard.)
HOWARD'S INFANTRY BATTALION. (Non-conscripts; also called 27th Battalion.)
Howard, T. B., Jr., major.
MCINTYRE'S BATTALION GEORGIA STATE GUARD. (Merged into 11th Regiment Georgia State Guard.)
McIntyre, A. T., major.
ORDNANCE BATTALION, Columbus, Ga.
Baldwin, W. W., major.
Oliveros, J. B., lieutenant-colonel.
PHILLIPS LEGION—INFANTRY BATTALION.
Barclay, E. Sandy, major, lieutenant-colonel.
Cook, Robert T., major, lieutenant-colonel.
Hamilton, Joseph, major, lieutenant-colonel.
Jones, Seaborn, Jr., lieutenant-colonel.
Norris, John S., major.
Phillips, William, colonel.
PHILLIPS LEGION—CAVALRY BATTALION.
Puckett, William B. C., major.
Rich, William W., lieutenant-colonel.
Willcoxon, John B., major.
ROSWELL BATTALION CAVALRY, LOCAL DEFENSE.
King, James R., major (acting.)
SMITH'S REGIMENT.. (Also called 1st Georgia Partisan Rangers; succeeded by Smith's Legion, composing an infantry and cavalry battalion, the infantry battalion becom-

ing 65th Infantry and cavalry battalion 6th Cavalry.)
    Smith, Sumner J., colonel.
SMITH'S LEGION.
    Smith, Sumner J., colonel.
SMITH'S LEGION—INFANTRY BATTALION.   (Merged into 65th In-
        fantry.)
    Fain, John S., lieutenant-colonel.
    Moore, Robert H., major.
SMITH'S LEGION—CAVALRY BATTALION.   (Merged into 6th Cav-
        alry.)
    Brown, Benjamin F., major.
    Hart, John R., lieutenant-colonel.
STEPHENS' CAVALRY BATTALION.   (See 7th Cavalry Battalion,
        Georgia State Guard.)
WICKER'S BATTALION.   (Merged into 12th Regiment Georgia
        State Guard.)
    Wicker, D. L., major.
WRIGHT'S CAVALRY REGIMENT GEORGIA STATE GUARD.   (Also
        called 12th.)
    Kenedy, James B., major.
    Longstreet, Anderson P., lieutenant-colonel.
    Wright, Henry G., colonel.
WRIGHT'S LEGION.   (See 38th Infantry.)
YOUNGBLOOD'S BATTALION GOVERNMENT MECHANICS, Columbus,
        Ga.
    Youngblood, E. H. (?), major.

ARTILLERY ORGANIZATIONS.

ATLANTA ARSENAL BATTERY.. Light Artillery.

Captain C. C. Campbell,	Appointed June 12, 1863.
Lieut. Wm. Hawksley,	Appointed June 12, 1863.
Lieut. L. S. Scruggs,	Appointed June 12, 1863.
2d Lieut. W. N. Cook,	Appointed June 12, 1863.
2d Lieut. Thos. E. Brady,	Appointed June 12, 1863.
Captain John H. Hudson,	Appointed February 1, 1864.
Lieut. L. S. Scruggs,	Appointed February 1, 1864.
Lieut. Thomas E. Brady,	Appointed February 1, 1864.
2d Lieut. M. Campbell,	Appointed February 1, 1864.
2d Lieut. W. D. West,	Appointed February 1, 1864.

AUGUSTA VOLUNTEER ARTILLERY. (See Barnes' Battery.)

BAKER'S BATTERY. Company State Troops for defense of Columbus, Ga.

Captain Robert. B. Baker,	Appointed July 5, 1864.
Lieut. David B. Caldwell,	Appointed July 5, 1864.
Lieut. Thomas M. Barnard,	Appointed July 5, 1864.
2d Lieut. James M. Clay,	Appointed July 5, 1864.
2d Lieut. John E. Thom,	Appointed July 5, 1864.

BARTOW ARTILLERY. (See A. C. Dunn's Battery, also Co. A, 22d Battalion.)

BARNES' BATTERY. Augusta Volunteer Artillery. Attached to 1st Regiment Local Volunteers, Col. G. W. Rains.

Captain George T. Barnes,	Appointed July 30, 1863.
Sr. Lieut. Jas. M. Roberts,	Appointed July 30, 1863.
Jr. Lieut. Charles Spaeth,	Appointed July 30, 1863.
2d Lieut. Robt. M. Phinizy,	Appointed July 30, 1863.
2d Lieut. R. J. Larcombe,	Appointed June 30, 1864.

BARNWELL'S BATTERY. 10th Battery, formerly D. A. Reese Battery.

Capt. A. Smith Barnwell,	Appointed March 12, 1864.
Lieut. John S. Acee,	Appointed March 12, 1864.
2d Lieut. Robert C. Jones,	Appointed March 12, 1864.
2d Lieut. Joseph A. Hill,	Appointed March 12, 1864.

BEN HILL ARTILLERY. See McLeod Artillery.

BEN HILL GUARDS.

BLACKSHEAR'S BATTERY.. (See Company D, Sumter Battalion.)

BLODGET'S FLYING ARTILLERY.

BLODGET'S VOLUNTEERS.

Originally Company I, 3d Infantry.

BLODGET'S BATTERY. . (Blodget Flying Artillery, or Blodget's
        Volunteers, afterward Milledge's Battery.)
        Captain Foster Blodget, Jr.,   Appointed August —, 1861.
        Sr. Lieut. Wm. H. Stallings,   Appointed August —, 1861.
        Jr. Lieut. Samuel Moore,   Appointed August —, 1861.
        2d Lieut. Augustus Speliers,   Appointed August —, 1861.
        2d Lieut. Jas. A. Bennett,   Appointed August —, 1861.

BROOKS' BATTERY. (See Terrell Artillery.)

BURTWELL'S BATTERY.—WASHINGTON ARTILLERY.   (Formerly
        Girardey's; after Pritchard's.)
        Captain J. R. B. Burtwell,   Appointed April 28, 1862.
                                      maj. arty., P. A. C. S.,
                                      June 23, 1863.
        Lieut. A. Speliers,   Appointed April 28, 1862.
        Lieut. Edward E. Pritchard,   Appointed April 28, 1862.
        2d Lieut. John Doscher,   Appointed April 28, 1862.
        2d Lieut. Robert Wallace,   Appointed April 28, 1862.

CALLAWAY'S (Lieutenant M.) BATTERY.. (Lieutenant Morgan
        Callaway was detached from Company B, Sumter,
        Georgia, Battalion, October 20, 1863, to command the
        Pulaski Artillery.)

CAMPBELL SIEGE ARTILLERY. (See C. G. Campbell's Battery.)

CAMPBELL'S (C. C.) BATTERY.. (See Atlanta Arsenal Battery.)

CAMPBELL'S (C. G.) BATTERY. (Campbell Siege Artillery.)
        Capt. Charles G. Campbell,   Appointed March 21, 1863.
        Lieut. B. F. Powell,   Appointed March 21, 1863.
        2d Lieut. J. T. Wimberly,   Appointed March 21, 1863.
        2d Lieut. W. C. Subers,   Appointed March 21, 1863.
        2d Lieut. G. W. Pearce,   Appointed Dec. 30, 1863.

CARLTON'S (Henry H.) BATTERY. (See Troup Artillery.)

CHATHAM ARTILLERY. (Detached from 1st Volunteers.)
        Capt. Joseph S. Claghorn,   Appointed August 1, 1861.
        Sr. Lieut. Chas. C. Jones, Jr., Appointed Aug. 1, 1861;
                                      maj. art'y, P. A. C. S.,
                                      Oct. 7, '62, and lt. col.
                                      art'y, P. A. C. S., Oct. 14,
                                      '62.
        Jr. Lieut. Julian Hartridge, Appointed August 1, 1861.

2d Lieut. Wm. M. Davidson,	Appointed August 1, 1861.
2d Lieut. Bernardino S. Sanchez,	Appointed August 1, 1861.
2d Lieut. Thomas A. Askew,	Appointed March 8, 1862.
Lieut. John F. Wheaton,	Appointed May 17, 1862.
2d Lieut. Samuel B. Palmer,	Appointed May 17, 1862.
Capt. John F. Wheaton,	Appointed Dec. 12, 1862.
Lieut. Thomas A. Askew,	Appointed Dec. 12, 1862.
Lieut. Samuel B. Palmer,	Appointed Dec. 12, 1862.
2d Lieut. Geo. A. Whitehead,	Appointed Dec. 12, 1862.
2d Lieut. George N. Hendry,	Appointed Dec. 22, 1862.

CHATHAM SIEGE ARTILLERY. Companies A and B, —— Battalion. (See S. O. A. and I. G. O., 1864; not identified.)

CHEROKEE ARTILLERY. Originally attached to 3d Infantry Battalion.

Capt. James G. Yeiser,	Appointed June 11, 1861; major art'y, P. A. C. S.
Sr. Lieut. Max Van Den Corput,	Appointed June 11, 1861.
2d Lieut. George W. Bowen,	Appointed June 11, 1861.
2d Lieut. Chas. O. Stillwell,	Appointed June 11, 1861.
Lieut. Meshack L. McWhorter,	Appointed April 1, 1862.
2d Lieut. William S. Hoge,	Appointed April 1, 1862.
Capt. Max Van Den Corput,	Appointed Dec. 31, 1862.
Lieut. Meshack L. McWhorter,	Appointed Dec. 31, 1862.
Lieut. William S. Hoge,	Appointed Dec. 31, 1862.
2d Lieut. John E. Stillwell,	Appointed Dec. 31, 1862.
2d Lieut. Wm. A. Russell,	Appointed Dec. 31, 1862.
2d Lieut. William L. Ritter,	Appointed August 31, 1863. Temporarily commanding detachment.

CHESTATEE ARTILLERY.. Detached from 38th Georgia Volunteers; ordered to rejoin May 5, 1864.

Capt. Thomas H. Bomar,	Appointed October 13, 1861.
Sr. Lieut. Truman H. Sanford,	Appointed October 13, 1861.
Jr. Lieut. Samuel E. Taylor,	Appointed October 13, 1861.
2d Lieut. John C. Hendrix,	Appointed October 13, 1861.
2d Lieut. William Hendrix,	Appointed April 19, 1862.
2d Lieut. J. F. Pigeon,	Appointed August 26, 1863.
Captain William Hendrix,	Appointed April 30, 1864.
Lieut. S. F. Crane,	Appointed April 30, 1864. Killed June 1, '64.
Lieut. J. O. McDaniel,	Appointed April 30, 1864.

CLINCH'S BATTERY.

Captain N. B. Clinch,	Appointed October 31, 1863.
Lieut. William P. Schirm,	Appointed October 31, 1863.
2d Lieut. R. C. Hazzard,	Appointed October 31, 1863.
2d Lieut. T. P. O'Neal,	Appointed October 31, 1863.

COBB GUARDS. (See Companies G and H, 22d Battalion.)

COLUMBUS LIGHT ARTILLERY.. Independent.

Captain Edward Croft,	Appointed Nov. 27, 1861.
Lieut. Alfred J. Young,	Appointed Nov. 27, 1861.
Lieut. George B. Young,	Appointed Dec. 5, 1861.
2d Lieut. William G. Croft,	Appointed Nov. 27, 1861.
2d Lieut. Warren J. John- son,	Appointed Nov. 27, 1861.
2d Lieut. M. D. Hornsby,	Appointed Sept 1, 1862.
Asst. Surg. T. H. Blount,	Appointed October —, 1862.

CORPUT'S BATTERY. (See Cherokee Artillery.)

CRAWFORD'S BATTERY.. (See Company C, Sumter Battalion.)

DANIELL'S BATTERY.

Captain Charles Daniell,	Appointed Dec. 21, 1863.
Lieut. John W. Magill,	Appointed Dec. 21, 1863.
2d Lieut. T. F. Daniell,	Appointed Dec. 21, 1863.
2d Lieut. John Y. Fraser,	Appointed Dec. 21, 1863.
2d Lieut. E. M. Weston,	Appointed Feb. 29, 1864.
2d Lieut. W. Barnwell,	Appointed August 31, 1864.

DAWSON'S (E. G.) BATTERY. (See Terrell Artillery.)

DAWSON'S (T. H.) BATTERY.. (See Company B, 14th Battalion.)

DUNN'S BATTERY. Originally Company A, 4th Georgia Battalion Infantry; afterward Company A, 60th Georgia Infantry.

Capt. Ambrose C. Dunn,	Appointed August 26, 1861.
Lieut. Benson W. Roberts,	Appointed August 26, 1861.
2d Lieut. J. M. Campbell,	Appointed August 26, 1861.
2d Lieut. G. S. Grace,	Appointed August 26, 1861.

DURE'S BATTERY. (See Jackson Artillery.)

ECHOLS LIGHT ARTILLERY.. Independent.

Captain J. H. Tiller,	Appointed March 4, 1862.
Lieut. W. M. Smith,	Appointed March 4, 1862.
Lieut. J. G. Gibson,	Appointed March 4, 1862.
2d Lieut. D. C. Smith,	Appointed March 4, 1862.
Lieut. Wm. H. Jarrell,	Appointed Dec. 13, 1862.
2d Lieut. James B. Wade,	Appointed Feb. 21, 1863.
2d Lieut. James M. Glenn,	Appointed April 15, 1863.

ELLS' BATTERY. (See Macon Light Artillery.)

EMMETT RIFLES.. (See Company F, 22d Battalion—Siege Artillery.)

ETOWAH IRON WORKS ARTILLERY.. (See Fay's Battery, State Troops.)

FAY'S BATTERY.. Etowah Iron Works Artillery, State Troops.

Captain Calvin Fay,   Appointed July 20, 1863.
Lieut. P. McLane,   Appointed July 20, 1863.
Lieut. J. W. Childs,   Appointed July 20, 1863.
2d Lieut. John Kirk, Jr.,   Appointed July 20, 1863.

FORREST ARTILLERY.. Company I, Floyd Legion, State Troops.

Captain C. O. Stillwell,   Appointed August —, 1863.
Lieut. C. H. Smith,   Appointed August —, 1863.
Lieut. J. M. Berry,   Appointed August —, 1863.
2d Lieut. Thomas F. Pierce,   Appointed August —, 1863.
2d Lieut. F. M. Ezzell,   Appointed August —, 1863.

NINTH BATTALION.

Major A. Leyden,   Appointed Feb. 27, 1862.
Surg. Noel d'Alvigny,   Appointed July 8, 1862, to rank from April 25, 1862.
Asst. Surg. Thos. E. Whyte,   Appointed April 26, 1864.
Adjutant George A. Lofton,   Appointed Sept. —, 1863.

COMPANY A. LEYDEN ARTILLERY.

Captain Elias Holcombe,   Appointed Feb. 27, 1862.
Lieut. William Barnes,   Appointed Feb. 27, 1862; captain July 23, 1863.
Lieut. Algernon S. Talley,   Appointed Feb. 27, 1862.
2d Lieut. George A. Lofton,   Appointed Feb. 27, 1862.
2d Lieut. Wm. R. McEntire,   Appointed Feb. 27, 1862.
2d Lieut. Benj. F. Wyly,   Appointed May 1, 1862; captain Co. E.

COMPANY B.

Capt. William W. Sentell,   Appointed March 4, 1862.
Lieut. Hardy J. Randall,   Appointed March 4, 1862; captain June 17, 1863.
Lieut. John Isom,   Appointed March 4, 1862.
2d Lieut. Edward H. Guess,   Appointed March 4, 1862.
2d Lieut. L. F. Heflin,   Appointed March 4, 1862.
2d Lieut. Uriah Owen,   Resignation accepted April 9, 1864.

COMPANY C.

Capt. Geo. W. Atkinson,   Appointed April 1, 1862.
Lieut. Thomas O. Douglass,   Appointed April 1, 1862.
Lieut. Andrew M. Wolihin,   Appointed April 1, 1862.
2d Lieut. Peter L. Key,   Appointed April 1, 1862.

Capt. Andrew M. Wollhin,	Appointed June 20, 1863.
Lieut. Peter L. Key,	Appointed June 20, 1863.
2d Lieut. Wm. W. Riden- hour,	Appointed July 9, 1863.
2d Lieut. Manly W. Ford,	Appointed July 9, 1863.
2d Lieut. W. W. Hall,	Appointed January 1, 1864.

COMPANY D. Gwinnett Artillery.

Capt. Tyler M. Peeples,	Appointed April 23, 1862.
Lieut. Wm. J. Born,	Appointed April 23, 1862.
Lieut. Thos. H. Loveless,	Appointed April 23, 1862.
2d Lieut. John T. Clower,	Appointed April 23, 1862.
2d Lieut. R. C. Montgomery,	Appointed April 23, 1862.

COMPANY E.

Capt. Benjamin F. Wyly,	Appointed March 15, 1862.
Lieut. Billington W. York,	Appointed March 15, 1862.
Lieut. William A. Haynes,	Appointed March 15, 1862.
2d Lieut. Wm. S. Everett,	Appointed March 15, 1862.
2d Lieut. Francis M. Blount,	Appointed March 15, 1862.
Capt. Billington W. York,	Appointed June 20, 1863.
Lieut. Wm. S. Everett,	Appointed June 20, 1863.
2d Lieut. Francis M. Blount,	Appointed June 20, 1863.
2d Lieut. W. R. Jackson,	Appointed June 20, 1863.

ELEVENTH BATTALION.   (See Sumter Battalion.)

TWELFTH BATTALION.

Major Henry D. Capers,	Appointed May 1, 1862; pro- moted lt. col. Nov. 6, '62.
Major George M. Hanvey,	Appointed Nov. 6, 1862.
Asst. Q.M. G. W. Crane,	Appointed May 1, 1862.
Asst. Q.M. C. W. Doughty,	Appointed August 29, 1862.
Asst. Com. Sub. Kerr Boyce,	Appointed January 12, 1863.
Adjutant F. W. Baker,	Appointed October 13, 1862; killed June 4, 1864.
Adjutant E. F. Clayton,	Appointed July 19, 1864.
Asst. Surg. B. F. Rudisill,	Appointed May 29, 1862.
Asst. Surg. C. B. Adams,	Appointed March 1, 1864.
Asst. Surg. S. H. Lamar,	Appointed May 1, 1864.

COMPANY A.

Capt. J. V. H. Allen,	Appointed April 10, 1862.
Lieut. Whitson G. Johnson,	Appointed April 10, 1862.
Lieut. L. A. Picquet,	Appointed April 10, 1862.
2d Lieut. Wilberforce Dan- iel,	Appointed April 10, 1862.
2d Lieut. A. W. Blanchard.	Appointed April 10, 1862.

Capt. George M. Hanvey,	Appointed May 26, 1862; Kennon Artillery.
Lieut. James W. Anderson,	Appointed May 26, 1862.
Lieut. Andrew P. Brown,	Appointed May 26, 1862.
2d Lieut. Josiah L. Mann,	Appointed May 26, 1862.
2d Lieut. Wm. S. Beadles,	Appointed May 26, 1862.
Capt. James W. Anderson,	Appointed Nov. 6, 1862.
Lieut. Andrew P. Brown,	Appointed Nov. 6, 1862; killed Oct. 27, '63.
Lieut. Josiah L. Mann,	Appointed Nov. 6, 1862; killed Sept. 19, '64.
2d Lieut. Wm. S. Beadles,	Appointed Nov. 6, 1862.
2d Lieut. David H. Brooks,	Appointed May 28, 1863; killed July 9, 1864.
2d Lieut. T. W. Anderson,	Appointed October 26, 1864.

COMPANY B (previous to October 1, 1862, was designated, according to roster, Company D; Newsome's company formed out of it, December 28, 1862.)

Capt. John W. Rudisill,	Appointed May 1, 1862.
Lieut. John J. Newsome,	Appointed May 1, 1862.
Lieut. H. T. Robson,	Appointed May 1, 1862.
2d Lieut. Geo. W. Peacock,	Appointed May 1, 1862.
2d Lieut. A. T. Sessions,	Appointed May 1, 1862; killed Oct. 19, 1864.
2d Lieut. J. K. Kinmon,	Appointed January 19, 1863.

COMPANY C. (Previous to October 1, 1862, was designated Company E, Captains Taliaferro's and Hood's companies formed out of it December 28, 1862.)

Capt. Samuel H. Crump,	Appointed May 1, 1862.
Lieut. Joseph N. Taliaferro,	Appointed May 1, 1862.
Lieut. George M. Hood,	Appointed May 1, 1862.
2d Lieut. Joshua J.Doughty,	Appointed May 1, 1862.
2d Lieut. A. M. MacMurphy,	Appointed May 1, 1862.

COMPANY D. (Previous to October 1, 1862, according to roster, designated as Company C; after December 28, 1862, appears as Company C again.)

Capt. George W. Johnson,	Appointed April 9, 1862.
Lieut. W. B. Wood,	Appointed April 9, 1862.
Lieut. M. L. Braden,	Appointed April 9, 1862.
2d Lieut. S. E. Brown,	Appointed April 9, 1862.
2d Lieut. F. W. Baker,	Appointed April 9, 1862.
Lieut. J. T. Willingham,	Appointed August 26, 1862.
Lieut. W. G. Head,	Appointed August 26, 1862; killed October 19, 1864.
2d Lieut. W. A. Goza,	Appointed January —, 1863.

2d Lieut. W. A. Scott,	Appointed Feb. —, 1863.
Asst. Surg. C. A. Rutledge,	Appointed January 29, 1863.
Capt. Joseph N. Taliaferro,	Appointed Dec. 23, 1862.
Lieut. C. W. Doughty,	Appointed January 19, 1863.
2d Lieut. Emanuel A. Nehr,	Appointed January 19, 1863.
2d Lieut. Sam'l Langley, Jr.,	Appointed January 19, 1863.

COMPANY E. (Formed out of Rudisill's company, December 28, 1862.)

Capt. John J. Newsome,	Appointed Dec. 28, 1862.
Lieut. George W. Peacock,	Appointed Dec. 28, 1862.
2d Lieut. James C. Smith,	Appointed January 19, 1863.
2d Lieut. Benj. S. Boatright,	Appointed January 19, 1863.

COMPANY F. (Formed out of Crump's company, December 28, 1862.)

Capt. George M. Hood,	Appointed Dec. 31, 1862.
Lieut. Joshua J. Doughty,	Appointed Dec. 31, 1862.
2d Lieut. John B. Alison,	Appointed January 19, 1863.
2d Lieut. Thomas J. Tutt,	Appointed Jan. 19, 1863; killed Oct. 19, 1864.

FOURTEENTH BATTALION. Serving with Robertson's 1st Battalion Reserve Artillery, Army of Tennessee, in 1863; Palmer's Battalion in 1864; Montgomery Artillery.

Major J. T. Montgomery,	Appointed April 15, 1862.
Major Joseph Palmer,	Appointed October 12, 1862.
Adjutant John H. Cox,	Appointed October 12, 1862.
Capt. and Com. Sub. Chas. T. Swift,	Appointed October 12, 1862.
Capt. & A. Q. M. James L. Moore,	Appointed June 7, 1862.
Asst. Surg. J. E. McMillan,	Appointed June 7, 1862.
Asst. Surg. Fred. A. Toomer,	Appointed May 6, 1862.
Asst. Surg. W. Reid Hurst,	Appointed Nov. 1, 1863.
Asst. Surg. Wm. H. Baxley,	Appointed Dec. 1, 1863.
Adjutant J. A. Byrd,	Appointed April 28, 1865.
Adjutant Benj. F Cameron,	Appointed May 12, 1862.

COMPANY A. Southern Rights Battery.

Captain Joseph Palmer,	Appointed April 26, 1862; adjutant.
Lieut. M. W. Havis,	Appointed April 26, 1862.
Lieut. James R. Duncan,	Appointed April 26, 1862.
2d Lieut. C. H. Smith,	Appointed April 26, 1862.
Capt. M. W. Havis,	Appointed October 12, 1862.
Lieut. James R. Duncan,	Appointed October 12, 1862.
Lieut. C. H. Smith,	Appointed October 12, 1862.

| 2d Lieut. James R. Rice, | Appointed October 12, 1862. |
| Lieut. Hamblin R. Felder, | Appointed June 30, 1863. |

COMPANY B. Pulaski Artillery.

Capt. Thomas H. Dawson,	Appointed April 15, 1862.
Lieut. R. W. Anderson,	Appointed April 15, 1862.
Lieut. Isaac O. Hall,	Appointed April 15, 1862.
2d Lieut. William Bembry,	Appointed April 15, 1862.
2d Lieut. Henry S. Greaves,	Appointed April 26, 1862.
Captain Sidney A. Moses,	Appointed March 1, 1863.
Capt. R. W. Anderson,	Appointed October 15, 1863.
Lieut. Henry S. Greaves,	Appointed October 15, 1863.
2d Lieut. Willis G. Allen,	Appointed Nov. 2, 1863.
2d Lieut. R. H. Brown,	Appointed Dec. 27, 1863.
2d Lieut. W. E. Hurst,	Attached Dec. 31, 1863.

COMPANY C.

Capt. C. B. Ferrell,	Appointed May 6, 1862.
Lieut. Wm. C. Henderson,	Appointed May 6, 1862.
Lieut. Sidney A. Moses,	Appointed May 6, 1862.
2d Lieut. James M. Truitt,	Appointed May 6, 1862.
2d Lieut. Benj. T. Cameron,	Appointed May 6, 1862.
Lieut. Nathan Davis,	Appointed Nov. 22, 1863.
2d Lieut. W. H. Ozburn,	Appointed Nov. 22, 1863.
Asst. Surg. W. C. Wheeler,	Appointed Dec. 5, 1863.
2d Lieut. John C. Battle,	Appointed Dec. —, 1864.

COMPANY D—Mountaineers.

Capt. E. R. King,	Appointed April 21, 1862.
Lieut. James G. Gibson,	Appointed April 21, 1862.
Lieut. M. W. Thweatt,	Appointed April 21, 1862.
2d Lieut. W. R. Beck,	Appointed April 21, 1862.
2d Lieut. W. B. S. Davis,	Appointed April 21, 1862.
2d Lieut. J. F. Brice,	Appointed October 6, 1862.

COMPANY E. (Clarke County Light Artillery; Arkansas Company, temporarily attached. (See Franklin Roberts' (Ark.) Battery.)

COMPANY F. Consolidated with Company D, December 5, 1862.

Capt. James G. Gibson,	Appointed October 7, 1862.
Lieut. Henry S. Greaves,	Appointed October 7, 1862.
2d Lieut. Wm. E. Hurst,	Appointed October 7, 1862.
2d Lieut. B. W. Roberts,	Appointed October 7, 1862.

COMPANY G. Stonewall Battery. Temporarily consolidated with Dawson's Battery March 1, 1863.

| Capt. Sidney A. Moses, | Appointed October 4, 1862. |
| Lieut. H. R. Felder, | Appointed October 4, 1862. |

Lieut. S. J. Howard,	Appointed October 4, 1862.
Lieut. R. W. Anderson,	Appointed Dec. 31, 1862.
2d Lieut. William Bembry,	Appointed Dec. 31, 1862.

TWENTY-SECOND BATTALION. Siege Artillery.

Lieut. Col. Wm. R. Pritchard,	Appointed October 13, 1862.
Major John B. Gallie,	Appointed October 29, 1862; killed February 1, 1863.
Major Mark J. McMullan,	Appointed Feb. 6, 1863.
Asst. Q. M. Edmund J. Dawson,	Appointed Nov. 28, 1862.
Asst. Q. M. Henry K. Washburn,	Appointed Dec. 20, 1863.
Adjutant John J. Symons,	Appointed Nov. 28, 1862; killed Feb. 18, 1863.
Adjutant Henry R. Symons,	Appointed Feb. 22, 1863.
Surgeon Joseph J. West,	Appointed ————, 1863.

COMPANY A. Bartow Artillery.

Capt. T. D. Bertody,	Appointed Dec. 10, 1861; promoted maj. art'y, P. A. C. S., April 25, 1863.
Lieut. A. B. Clarke,	Appointed Dec. 10, 1861.
2d Lieut. J. M. Campbell,	Appointed Dec. 10, 1861.
2d Lieut. G. S. Grace,	Appointed Dec. 10, 1861.
2d Lieut. George R. Niles,	Appointed Dec. 31, 1861.
2d Lieut. C. C. Campbell,	Appointed Feb. 13, 1863.
Capt. J. M. Campbell,	Appointed March 25, 1863.
Lieut. George R. Niles,	Appointed March 25, 1863.
2d Lieut. C. C. Campbell,	Appointed March 25, 1863.
2d Lieut. J. S. Knott,	Appointed May 18, 1863.
Capt. George R. Niles,	Appointed Feb. —, 1864.
Lieut. C. C. Campbell,	Appointed Feb. —, 1864.
2d Lieut. J. S. Knott,	Appointed Feb. —, 1864.
2d Lieut. E. P. Halsted,	Appointed Feb. —, 1864.

COMPANY B. Wise Guards. Originally Co. K, 25th Ga. Infantry.

Capt. Mark J. McMullan,	Appointed Sept. 2, 1861.
Lieut. T. W. Montfort,	Appointed Sept. 2, 1861.
2d Lieut. J. D. N. Sutton,	Appointed Sept. 2, 1861.
2d Lieut. John H. Blow,	Appointed Sept. 2, 1861.
Lieut. D. A. Smith,	Appointed October 1, 1862.
2d Lieut. James W. Holt,	Appointed October 1, 1862.
Captain D. A. Smith,	Appointed Feb. 6, 1863.
Lieut. John H. Blow,	Appointed Feb. 6, 1863.
2d Lieut. James W. Holt,	Appointed Feb. 6, 1863.

2d Lieut. H. F. Tarrer,	Appointed March 27, 1863.
2d Lieut. Wm. S. Williams,	Appointed July 11, 1863.
2d Lieut. James L. Milton,	Appointed October 14, 1863.
2d Lieut. Julius Turner,	Appointed Nov. 25, 1863.
2d Lieut. John B. Mathis,	Appointed Dec. 22, 1863.

COMPANY C. Originally Co. A, Oglethorpe Siege Artillery Battalion.

Capt. John Lama,	Appointed May 14, 1862.
Lieut. Algernon S. Hartridge,	Appointed May 14, 1862.
2d Lieut. Joseph A. Beals,	Appointed May 14, 1862.
2d Lieut. Thomas W. Neely,	Appointed May 14, 1862.
2d Lieut. Frederick Dietz,	Appointed July 1, 1862.
2d Lieut. Alex. Campbell,	Appointed Feb. 28, 1863.
Capt. Joseph A. Beals,	Appointed October 31, 1863.
Lieut. Frederick Dietz,	Appointed October 31, 1863.
2d Lieut. Alexander Campbell,	Appointed October 31, 1863.
2d Lieut. Joseph Coupe,	Appointed October 31, 1863.
2d Lieut. Milton C. Wade,	Appointed March 1, 1864.

COMPANY D. Originally Co. B, Oglethorpe Siege Artillery Battalion.

Capt. R. J. Nunn,	Appointed July 29, 1862.
Lieut. James Manning,	Appointed July 29, 1862.
Lieut. Joseph T. Steele,	Appointed July 29, 1862.
2d Lieut. O. S. Perry,	Appointed July 29, 1862.
2d Lieut. Dudley Kelly,	Appointed Jan. 10, 1863.
Capt. James Manning,	Appointed April 3, 1863.
Lieut. O. S. Perry,	Appointed April 3, 1863.
2d Lieut. Dudley Kelly,	Appointed April 3, 1863.
2d Lieut. Martin Helmkin,	Appointed April 11, 1863.

COMPANY E. Montgomery Guards. Originally Capt. Lawrence J. Guilmartin's Infantry company attached to 1st Vol. Ga. Infantry.

Capt. Christopher Hussey,	Appointed October 9, 1862.
Lieut. Thomas Houlihan,	Appointed October 9, 1862.
2d Lieut. Christopher, Murphy,	Appointed October 9, 1862.
2d Lieut. Maurice Crowley,	Appointed October 9, 1862.
2d Lieut. B. M. Neely,	Appointed Jan. 1, 1864.
2d Lieut. J. E. Holmes,	Appointed August 16, 1864.

COMPANY F. Emmett Rifles. Originally attached to 1st Vol. Regiment Georgia Infantry.

Capt. A. Bonaud,	Appointed Feb. 6, 1862.
Lieut. W. E. Long, Jr.,	Appointed Feb. 6, 1862.

2d Lieut. G. W. Dickerson,	Appointed Feb. 6, 1862.
2d Lieut. W. S. Rockwell, Jr.,	Appointed Feb. 6, 1862.
Capt. George A. Nicoll,	Appointed October 31, 1862.
Lieut. G. W. Dickerson,	Appointed October 31, 1862.
Lieut. W. S. Rockwell, Jr.,	Appointed October 31, 1862.
2d Lieut. Daniel Quinn,	Appointed October 31, 1862.
2d Lieut. Edgar M. McDonnell,	Appointed Dec. 31, 1862.

COMPANY G. Cobb Guards. Co. A; temporarily attached September 19, 1863.

Capt. Francis T. Cullens,	Appointed Sept. 19, 1863.
Lieut. Alex. R. Baugh,	Appointed Sept. 19, 1863.
2d Lieut. John L. Yarborough,	Appointed Sept. 19, 1863.
2d Lieut. Burrell Taylor,	Appointed Sept. 24, 1863.

COMPANY H. Cobb Guards, (Co. B.), temporarily attached Sept. 19, 1863.)

Capt. Rich'rd A. Turnipseed,	Appointed Sept. 19, 1863.
Lieut. John C. Wells,	Appointed Sept. 19, 1863.
2d Lieut. Wm. J. Weems,	Appointed Sept. 19, 1863.
2d Lieut. Rufus M. Johnson,	Appointed Sept. 19, 1863.
2d Lieut. Benj. F. McCarty,	Appointed April 12, 1864.

TWENTY-EIGHTH BATTALION. Organized as Siege Artillery; after January, 1864, serving as infantry.

Major A. Bonaud,	Appointed August 6, 1863.
Adjutant Robert Knox,	Appointed August 6, 1863; killed July 9, 1864.
Adjutant W. C. Riesberg,	Appointed July 22, 1864.
Asst. Q.M. W. E. Long, Jr.,	Appointed August 6, 1863.
Asst. Surg. E. Tison,	Appointed Nov. 10, 1863.
Asst. Surg. R. J. Perry,	Appointed Nov. 14, 1864.

COMPANY A.

Capt. Joseph A. Cotten,	Appointed July 15, 1863.
Lieut. George C. Beale,	Appointed July 15, 1863.
2d Lieut. Julius Gardner,	Appointed July 15, 1863.
2d Lieut. W. F. Mason,	Appointed July 15, 1863.
2d Lieut. W. J. Largen,	Appointed Dec. 5, 1863.

COMPANY B.

Capt. D. B. Fickling,	Appointed August 1, 1863.
Lieut. T. J. Key,	Appointed August 1, 1863.
2d Lieut. H. W. Stevens,	Appointed August 1, 1863.
2d Lieut. A. B. Stroud,	Appointed August 1, 1863.
2d Lieut. F. J. Abbott,	Appointed May 30, 1864.
2d Lieut. L. G. Davis,	Appointed Nov. 1, 1864.
2d Lieut. Wm. Warlick,	Appointed Nov. 19, 1864.

COMPANY C.

Capt. Chas. P. Crawford,	Appointed August 5, 1863.
Lieut. Julien Ransone,	Appointed August 5, 1863.
Lieut. Thomas M. Allen,	Appointed August 5, 1863.
2d Lieut. Burrell J. Kendrick,	Appointed August 5, 1863.

COMPANY D.

Capt. Jordan Wilcher,	Appointed August 6, 1863.
Lieut. Thaddeus Oliver,	Appointed August 6, 1863; died Aug. 20, 1864, of wounds received in battle.
2d Lieut. James W. Hall,	Appointed August 6, 1863.
2d Lieut. H. H. Hunter,	Appointed August 6, 1863.
2d Lieut. John H. Blow,	Appointed July 27, 1864.

COMPANY E.

Capt. Malcolm T. McGregor,	Appointed August 20, 1863; maj. art'y, P. A. C. S., March 1, 1865.
Lieut. James A. McGregor,	Appointed August 20, 1863.
2d Lieut. Jno. W. Johnston,	Appointed August 20, 1863.
2d Lieut. Willis Newton,	Appointed August 20, 1863.

COMPANY F.

Captain James R. Blount,	Appointed Sept. 4, 1863.
Lieut. J. T. Price,	Appointed Sept. 4, 1863.
2d Lieut. W. J. Tooke,	Appointed Sept. 4, 1863.
2d Lieut. Thomas Ribero,	Appointed Sept. 4, 1863; killed at Chickamauga.
2d Lieut. W. H. Hicks,	Appointed April 7, 1864.

COMPANY G. Yancy Siege Artillery.

Capt. John D. Godwin,	Appointed Sept. 14, 1863.
Lieut. Cader Pierce,	Appointed Sept. 14, 1863.
2d Lieut. W. B. Whithurst,	Appointed Sept. 14, 1863.
2d Lieut. Jas. W. Lawrence,	Appointed Sept. 14, 1863.

COMPANY H. Formerly Co. C, 20th Ala. Battalion Artillery.

Capt. Thomas J. Key,	Appointed Jan. 1, 1864.
Lieut. Wm. A. Farley,	Appointed Jan. 1, 1864.
2d Lieut. W. T. Black,	Appointed Jan. 1, 1864.
2d Lieut. L. F. McCoy,	Appointed Jan. 1, 1864.

COMPANY I.

Capt. B. F. Bishop,	Appointed April 16, 1863.
Lieut. W. A. Ragsdale,	Appointed April 16, 1863.
2d Lieut. Robert C. Irwin,	Appointed April 16, 1863.
2d Lieut. John T. Walton,	Appointed Nov. 6, 1863.

COMPANY K. Mercer Artillery.

Capt. A. J. Macarthy,	Appointed Nov. 2, 1863.
Lieut. John W. Flint,	Appointed Nov. 2, 1863.
2d Lieut. A. N. Hines,	Appointed Nov. 2, 1863.
2d Lieut. A. K. Jennings,	Appointed Nov. 2, 1863.

GEORGIA LIGHT ARTILLERY. State Troops. Disbanded May 30, 1862. No rolls on file.

Capt. Horatio N. Hollifield, Promoted surgeon.

GEORGIA REGULARS. Co. A, 1st Regulars. (See S. P. Hamilton's Battery, Co. D, 1st Regulars; see Jacob Read's and J. A. Maxwell's Batteries.)

GIBSON'S (O. C.) BATTERY. (See Griffin Light Artillery.)

GIRARDEY'S (Isadore P.) BATTERY. (See Washington Artillery.)

GRIFFIN LIGHT ARTILLERY. Also called Church Bell Artillery.

Capt. Obadiah C. Gibson,	Appointed May 7, 1862.
Lieut. John Scogin,	Appointed May 7, 1862.
Lieut. Hardy C. Fryer,	Appointed May 7, 1862.
2d Lieut. Robert J. Powell,	Appointed May 7, 1862.
Capt. John Scogin,	Appointed Sept. —, 1862.
Lieut. Robert J. Powell,	Appointed Sept. —, 1862.
2d Lieut. Wm. E. Lyons,	Appointed Sept. —, 1862.
2d Lieut. Geo. M. Rockwell,	Appointed Dec. —, 1862.
2d Lieut. Joshua J. Head,	Appointed October 7, 1863.

GUERARD'S BATTERY.

Capt. John M. Guerard,	Appointed Sept. 8, 1863.
Lieut. John A. McManus,	Appointed Sept. 8, 1863.
Lieut. Wm. Robt. Gignilliat,	Appointed Sept. 8, 1863.
Lieut. John B. Lewis,	Appointed October 16, 1863
Lieut. Wm. E. Guerard,	Appointed March 16, 1864.

GWINNETT ARTILLERY. (See Company D, 9th Battalion.)

HAMILTON'S (S. P.) BATTERY. Company A, 1st Georgia Regulars. Organized as artillery July 24, 1861; disbanded July 15, 1862, and men transferred to 1st Georgia Regulars.

Captain S. P. Hamilton,	Appointed July 24, 1861; promoted maj. art'y July 14, 1862.
Lieut. Robert A. Crawford,	Appointed July 24, 1861.
Lieut. Thomas A. Maddox,	Appointed July 24, 1861.
2d Lieut. John Lane,	Appointed August 16, 1861; by transfer; major artillery, April 4, 1863, and lieutenant - colonel artillery, March 1, 1865.

Lieut. Edmund Taylor,	Appointed Nov. —, 1861; temporarily assigned. Maj.
Lieut. J. Floyd King,	Appointed Nov. —, 1861; temporarily assigned maj. arty., July 22, '62; and lieutenant colonel arty., Sept. 3, 1863.
2d Lieut. William A. Deas,	Appointed Feb. 9, 1862.
2d Lieut. Frank Steiner,	Appointed Feb. 9, 1862.

HAVIS BATTERY. (See Company A, 14th Battalion.)

HILL'S BATTERY.—Capt. A. A. Franklin Hill, commanding battery April 8, 1861; afterwards captain of companies A and M, 1st Georgia Regulars, and major of same regiment.

HOWELL'S BATTERY. (Formerly R. Martin's Battery.)

Capt. Evan P. Howell,	Appointed Sept. 7, 1863.
Lieut. W. G. Robson,	Appointed Sept. 7, 1863.
2d Lieut. T. J. Gilmore,	Appointed Sept. 7, 1863.
2d Lieut. R. T. Gibson,	Appointed Sept. 7, 1863.

HUDSON'S (J. H.) BATTERY. (See Atlanta Arsenal Battery.)

HURT LIGHT ARTILLERY.
Lieut. Joseph A. Alexander,

JACKSON ARTILLERY.

Capt. George A. Dure,	Appointed Sept. 18, 1861.
Lieut. Ebenezer C. Grier,	Appointed Sept. 18, 1861.
Lieut. Chas. F. Stubbs,	Appointed Sept. 18, 1861.
2d Lieut. T. L. Massenburg,	Appointed Sept. 18, 1861.
Lieut. J. F. Greer,	Appointed May 17, 1862.
2d Lieut. J. A. Holtzclaw,	Appointed May 17, 1862.
Capt. Thos. L. Massenburg,	Appointed Feb. 21, 1863.
Lieut. J. F. Greer,	Appointed Feb. 21, 1863.
2d Lieut. J. A. Holtzclaw,	Appointed Feb. 21, 1863.
2d Lieut. George B. Foster,	Appointed Feb. 21, 1863; killed at Mission'ry Ridge.
2d Lieut. R. G. Burgess,	Appointed July 17, 1863; killed Aug. 12, 1864.

JO. THOMPSON ARTILLERY. Originally Company M, 38th Georgia Infantry.

Capt. Lewis J. Parr,	Appointed Sept. 26, 1861.
Lieut. C. R. Hanleiter,	Appointed Sept. 26, 1861.
2d Lieut. Elijah J. Craven,	Appointed Sept. 26, 1861.
2d Lieut. Wm. P. McDaniel,	Appointed Sept. 26, 1861.
Capt. Cornelius R. Hanleiter,	Appointed October 25, 1861.
Lieut. Elijah J. Craven,	Appointed October 25, 1861.

Lieut. Wm. P. McDaniel,	Appointed October 25, 1861.
Lieut. Augustus Shaw,	Appointed October 25, 1861.
Lieut. Wm. R. Hanleiter,	Appointed Nov. 19, 1862.
2d Lieut. Thos. A. Kenady,	Appointed Dec. 5, 1862.
2d Lieut. James T. Peacock,	Appointed Feb. 21, 1863.
Surgeon J. H. Houston,	Appointed March 16, 1863.

LAMA'S BATTERY. (See Company A, Oglethorpe Siege Artillery Battalion; also Company C, 22d Georgia Battalion.)

LANE'S BATTERY. (See Company C, Sumter Battalion.)

LATHAM'S BATTERY. State Troops; at Columbus, Ga., December —, 1863.

Captain Woodville Latham, appointed.

LEYDEN ARTILLERY. (See Company A, 9th Battalion.)

LUMPKIN'S BATTERY.

Capt. E. P. Lumpkin,	Appointed Feb. 1, 1864.
Lieut. W. C. Wier,	Appointed Feb. 1, 1864.
Lieut. W. H. Morton,	Appointed Feb. 1, 1864.
Lieut. S. W. Prewit,	Appointed Feb. 1, 1864.
2d Lieut. A. G. Turner,	Appointed Feb. 1, 1864.

McLEOD ARTILLERY. Originally Company C, 38th Infantry (Wright's Legion); afterward Ben Hill Artillery, which was permanently detached from 38th Georgia Infantry, May 5, 1864.

Capt. Wm. L. McLeod,	Appointed October 1, 1861.
Lieut. Miller A. Wright,	Appointed October 1, 1861.
2d Lieut. John A. Williamson,	Appointed October 1, 1861.
2d Lieut. Jacob P. Pugsley,	Appointed October 1, 1861.
2d Lieut. John B. Higdon,	Appointed October 31, 1862; captain October 31, 1863.
2d Lieut. Benj. T. Morris,	Appointed August 31, 1863.

MACON LIGHT ARTILLERY. Formerly Napier Artillery.

Capt. H. N. Ells,	Appointed May 3, 1862.
Lieut. W. F. Anderson,	Appointed May 3, 1862.
Lieut. H. A. Troutman,	Appointed May 3, 1862.
2d Lieut. C. W. Slaten,	Appointed May 3, 1862.
2d Lieut. F. M. Folds,	Appointed May 3, 1862.
Capt. C. W. Slaten,	Appointed June 6, 1863.
Lieut. F. M. Folds,	Appointed June 6, 1863.
Lieut. H. M. Varner,	Appointed June 6, 1863.

MARTIN LIGHT ARTILLERY. (See Robert Martin's Battery.)

MARTIN'S BATTERY. Martin Light Artillery; after Howell's.

Capt. Robert Martin,	Appointed May 10, 1862; major art'y, Sept. 7, 1863.

Lieut. Evan P. Howell,	Appointed May 10, 1862; captain.
Lieut. W. G. Robson,	Appointed May 10, 1862.
2d Lieut. U. M. Erwin,	Appointed May 10, 1862.
2d Lieut. R. H. Bland,	Appointed May 10, 1862.
2d Lieut. T. J. Gilmore,	Appointed August, 1863.
2d Lieut. R. T. Gibson,	Appointed August, 1863.

MAXWELL ARTILLERY. Company D, 1st Georgia Regulars; formerly J. Read's Battalion; after Guerard's Battalion, February 28, 1863.

Capt. J. A. Maxwell,	Appointed Feb. 28, 1863.
Lieut. J. M. Guerard,	Appointed Feb. 28, 1863; captain.
Lieut. J. A. Huger,	Appointed Feb. 28, 1863.
2d Lieut. C. B. Richardson,	Appointed June 30, 1863.
2d Lieut. John B. Elliott,	Appointed June 30, 1863.
Asst. Surg. H. H. Harley,	Appointed June 30, 1863.

MERCER ARTILLERY. (See Company K, 28th Battalion.)

MILLEDGE ARTILLERY. Pendleton Light Artillery; formerly Blodget's Battery. One section of Blackshear's Battery assigned October 4, 1862.

Capt. John Milledge, Jr.,	Appointed May —, 1862.
Lieut. John T. Rodgers,	Appointed May —, 1862.
Lieut. Hardy H. Fulghum,	Appointed May —, 1862.
2d Lieut. Jesse Thompson,	Appointed May —, 1862.
Lieut. Thos. A. Maddox,	Appointed October 4, 1862.
2d Lieut. Robert Falligant,	Appointed October 4, 1862.

MILLEDGE'S BATTERY. (See Milledge's Artillery.)

MONTGOMERY ARTILLERY. (See 14th Battalion.)

MONTGOMERY GUARDS. (See Company E, 22d Battalion; originally Guilmartin's Infantry company, attached to 1st Vol. Ga. Regiment.)

MOSES' BATTERY. . (See Company G, 14th Battalion. Temporarily consolidated with Company B, March 1, 1863.)

MOUNTAINEERS.. (See Company D, 14th Battalion.)

NAPIER ARTILLERY. (Afterward Macon Light Artillery.)

| Capt. Leroy Napier, Jr., | Appointed Jan. 1, 1862; lt.-col. 8th Ga. Batt. Inf.; 1st lieut. of art'y, June 6, 1861. |
| Lieut. H. N. Ells, | Appointed Jan. 1, 1862; capt. Macon Light Art'y. |

NEWNAN ARTILLERY. Hanvey's Battery. (See Company A, 12th Battalion.)

NUNN'S BATTERY. (See Company B, Oglethorpe Siege Artillery; also Company D, 22d Battalion.)

OGLETHORPE ARTILLERY. Company —, 8th Georgia Volunteers, as given in local designation. (Not to be included in artillery organization.)

OGLETHORPE LIGHT ARTILLERY. Company A, 63d Georgia Infantry, as given in local designation. (Not to be included in artillery organization.)

OGLETHORPE SIEGE ARTILLERY BATTALION.
COMPANY A—(See Company C, 22d Battalion.)
COMPANY B—(See G. F. Oliver's Battery; see also Company D, 22d Battalion.)

OLIVER'S BATTERY. Company B, Oglethorpe Siege Artillery Battalion; afterward Nunn's Battery.

Capt. G. F. Oliver,	Appointed May 22, 1862.
Lieut. R. J. Nunn,	Appointed May 22, 1862.
Lieut. James Manning,	Appointed May 22, 1862.
2d Lieut. Joseph T. Steele,	Appointed May 22, 1862.

PATTERSON'S (G. M.) BATTERY. (See Company B, Sumter Battalion.)

PEEPLES BATTERY. (See Gwinnett Artlilery, Co. D, 9th Battalion.)

PRICE'S (J. V.) BATTERY. (See Company B, Sumter Battalion.)

PRITCHARD'S BATTERY. Formerly Burtwell's and Girardey's.

Capt. Edward E. Pritchard,	Appointed August 25, 1862.
Lieut. Robert Wallace,	Appointed August 25, 1862.
Lieut. John Doscher,	Appointed August 25, 1862.
2d Lieut. James M. Roberts,	Appointed August 25, 1862.
2d Lieut. Rich'd Summerall,	Appointed April 21, 1863.

PULASKI ARTILLERY. Also called Pulaski Guards. Originally Company K, 10th Georgia Infantry. Temporarily attached to 1st Virginia Artillery.

Capt. John P. W. Read,	Appointed June 18, 1861; maj. art'y April 4, 1863; lt.-col. art'y, Nov. 5, 1864.
Lieut. John M. Millen,	Appointed June 18, 1861.
2d Lieut. Geo. H. Cheever,	Appointed June 18, 1861.
2d Lieut. John C. Fraser,	Appointed June 18, 1862; captain March 2, 1863.
2d Lieut. Sam'l B. Parkman,	Appointed Dec. 31, 1861; killed Sept. 17, 1862.
2d Lieut. Wm. J. Furlong,	Appointed June 1, 1862.
2d Lieut. Frederick A. Habersham,	Appointed Feb. 7, 1863.

2d Lieut. R. H. Couper,	Appointed April —, 1863.
Lieut. Morgan Callaway,	Appointed October 20, 1863; commanding.
2d Lieut. Hugh Young,	Appointed July 30, 1864.

READ'S BATTERY. Company D, 1st Georgia Regulars, appears organized as artillery November, 1861; after Maxwell's Battery.

Capt. Jacob Read,	Appointed Nov. 1, 1861.
Lieut. A. B. Montgomery,	Appointed Nov. 1, 1861.
2d Lieut. J. A. Maxwell,	Appointed Nov. 1, 1861.
2d Lieut. John M. Guerard,	Appointed Nov. 1, 1861; promoted captain art'y.
2d Lieut. H. Bechter,	Appointed July 1, 1862.
2d Lieut. Jos. A. Huger, Jr.,	Appointed July 6, 1862.
Asst. Surg. W. K. Fort,	Appointed July 11, 1862.
Capt. J. A. Maxwell,	Appointed Feb. 1, 1863.
Lieut. John M. Guerard,	Appointed Feb. 1, 1863.
Lieut. Jos. A. Huger, Jr.,	Appointed Feb. 1, 1863.
2d Lieut. C. B. Richardson,	Appointed May 20, 1863.
2d Lieut. John B. Elliott,	Appointed May 23, 1863.
Asst. Surg. H. H. Harley,	Appointed May 31, 1863.

READ'S (J. P. W.) BATTERY. (See Pulaski Artillery). Originally Company K, 10th Georgia Infantry. (Attached as Company K or L to 1st Virginia Artillery.)

RICE'S (J. V.) BATTERY. (See Company B, Sumter Battalion.)

REGULAR LIGHT BATTERY. (See Maxwell's Artillery.)

RESERVE CHATHAM ARTILLERY.

RITTER'S (W. L.) BATTERY. (See Stephens Light Artillery, Ga. Volunteers.)

Capt. W. L. Ritter,	Appointed Dec. 16, 1864.

ROSS' (H. M.) BATTERY. (See Company A, Sumter Battalion.)

SAVANNAH ARTILLERY. Originally attached to 1st Vol. Reg. Ga. Infantry.

Capt. John B. Gallie,	Appointed May 31, 1861.
Lieut. Claudius C. Wilson,	Appointed May 31, 1861.
Lieut. John Lama,	Appointed May 31, 1861.
2d Lieut. Geo. L. Cope,	Appointed May 31, 1861.

SOUTHERN RIGHTS BATTERY. (See Company A, 14th Battalion.)

STANLEY'S (M.) BATTERY. (See Troup Artillery.)

STEPHENS' LIGHT ARTILLERY.

NOTE.—Prior to November 13, 1863, this command constituted the 3d Maryland Battery.

STONEWALL BATTERY. (See Company G, 14th Battalion.)

SUMTER BATTALION. (Eleventh Battalion.)

Major Allen S. Cutts,	Appointed May 22, 1862; lieut.-col. art'y, May 26, 1862; col. art'y, April 22, 1864.
Major John Lane,	Appointed March 2, 1863; major art'y, April 4, 1863; lieut.-colonel art'y, March 1, 1865.
Surgeon W. A. Greene,	Appointed June 12, 1862.
Surgeon Henry F. Andrews,	Appointed October —, 1864.
Asst. Surg. John W. Hill,	Appointed June 27, 1862.
Asst. Surg. Jas. B. Gilkeson,	Appointed April 21, 1863.
Chaplain Joseph S. Brown,	Appointed Sept. 30, 1862.
Chaplain W. M. Davis,	Appointed Dec. 12, 1863.
Asst. Com. Sub. Frank Arnold,	Appointed August 11, 1862.
Asst. Q.M. T. H. Johnston,	Appointed May 22, 1862.
Asst. Q.M. Wm. E. Duncan,	Appointed October 31, 1863.
Asst. Q.M. Jas. M. Goodman,	Appointed Nov. 14, 1863.
Asst. Q.M. J. B. Jett,	Appointed Sept. 3, 1864.
Adjutant F. M. Coker,	Appointed July 19, 1862.
Adj. Malcolm B. Council,	Appointed June 9, 1863.
Ordnance Officer Joseph T. Allyn,	Appointed October 31, 1863.

COMPANY A. Formerly Cutts' Battery. Sumter Flying Artillery.

Capt. Hugh M. Ross,	Appointed May 23, 1862. maj. arty. March 1, 1865.
Lieut. Lucius G. Rees,	Appointed May 23, 1862.
Lieut. Bryan James,	Appointed May 23, 1862.
2d Lieut. L. E. Spivey,	Appointed May 23, 1862.
2d Lieut. Eli K. Bozeman,	Appointed May 23, 1862; captain Feb. 8, 1865.
2d Lieut. H. D. Randall,	Appointed Sept. 8, 1864.
2d Lieut. Thos. S. Greene,	Appointed Nov. 25, 1864.

COMPANY B. Consolidated with Company C, July 19, 1862.

Capt. John V. Price,	Appointed April 16, 1862.
Lieut. F. M. Coker,	Appointed April 16, 1862.
Lieut. J. H. P. Murray,	Appointed April 16, 1862.
2d Lieut. Geo. M. Patterson,	Appointed April 16, 1862.
2d Lieut. Micajah J. Harper,	Appointed April 16, 1862.
Capt. Geo. M. Patterson,	Appointed July 21, 1862.
Lieut. Morgan Callaway,	Appointed July 21, 1862.
Lieut. Zadok Jackson,	Appointed July 21, 1862.

67

2nd Lieut. John P. Duncan,	Appointed July 21, 1862.
2d Lieut. Micajah J. Harper,	Appointed July 21, 1862.
2d Lieut. J. H. Pullen,	Appointed Sept. 17, 1864.
2d Lieut. H. H. Harvay,	Appointed October 30, 1864.

COMPANY C. Consolidated with Company B, July 19, 1862.

Capt. C. P. Crawford,	Appointed April 16, 1862.
Lieut. J. M. R. Westbrook,	Appointed April 16, 1862.
Lieut. W. L. Mann,	Appointed April 16, 1862.
2d Lieut. Zadok Jackson,	Appointed April 16, 1862.
2d Lieut. J. H. Bailey,	Appointed April 16, 1862.

COMPANY D. Disbanded October 4, 1862, and men assigned to Ross', Lane's and Patterson's companies.

Capt. Jas. Ap. Blackshear,	Appointed May 15, 1862; conscript service.
Lieut. J. W. Walker,	Appointed May 15, 1862; died July 2, 1862.
Lieut. Malcolm B. Council,	Appointed May 15, 1862; adjutant.
2d Lieut. J. L. Wilson,	Appointed May 15, 1862.
2d Lieut. W. T. Sadler,	Appointed May 15, 1862.
Lieut. J. M. R. Westbrook,	Appointed August 15, 1862.
2d Lieut. E. H. Winn,	Appointed August 15, 1862.
Lieut. Thomas A. Maddox,	Appointed October —, 1862.

COMPANY E. Originally Company A, 9th Georgia Infantry. Irwin Artillery.

Capt. John Lane,	Appointed Dec. 13, 1861.
Lieut. John T. Wingfield,	Appointed Dec. 13, 1861.
Lieut. Thos. P. Furgerson,	Appointed Dec. 13, 1861.
2d Lieut. Frank Arnold,	Appointed Dec. 13, 1861.
2d Lieut. Felix T. Griffin,	Appointed Dec. 13, 1861.
2d Lieut. Jos. W. Barnett,	Appointed May 1, 1862.
2d Lieut. G. Andrews,	Appointed October 1, 1862.
Capt. John T. Wingfield,	Appointed March 2, 1863.
Lieut. Frank Arnold,	Appointed March 2, 1863.
Lieut. Felix T. Griffin,	Appointed March 2, 1863.
2d Lieut. Jos. W. Barnett,	Appointed March 2, 1863.
2d Lieut. Chas. E. Irwin,	Appointed March 2, 1863.
2d Lieut. R. A. Harris,	Appointed Sept. 20, 1864.

SUMTER FLYING ARTILLERY. Afterward Ross' Battery, Company A, Sumter (11th) Battalion.

Capt. Allen S. Cutts,	Appointed July 15, 1861.
Lieut. Hugh M. Ross,	Appointed July 15, 1861.
Lieut. George F. Smith,	Appointed July 15, 1861.
2d Lieut. Samuel Heys,	Appointed July 15, 1861.
Asst. Surg. Bedford J. Head,	Appointed July 15, 1861.

Lieut. Bryan James,	Appointed Nov. 1, 1861.
Lieut. L. E. Spivey,	Appointed Nov. 1, 1861.
2d Lieut. Lucius G. Rees,	Appointed Jan. 1, 1862.

TERRELL LIGHT ARTILLERY.

Capt. Edgar G. Dawson,	Appointed Sept. 27, 1861; maj. art'y April 25, 1863.
Lieut. John W. Brooks,	Appointed Sept. 27, 1861.
Lieut. Chas. Wright,	Appointed Sept. 27, 1861.
2d Lieut. Thos. M. Barnard,	Appointed Sept. 27, 1861
2d Lieut. John B. Pouncey,	Appointed Dec. 12, 1862.
2d Lieut. D. M. Gurley,	Appointed May 25, 1863.
2d Lieut. E. W. Stoker,	Appointed May 4, 1864.

TROUP ARTILLERY. Originally attached to 2d Georgia Infantry; afterward with Cobb's Georgia Legion.

Capt. Marcellus Stanley,	Appointed April 24, 1861; maj. art'y Jan. 2, 1863.
Lieut. Henry H. Carlton,	Appointed April 24, 1861. Captain Apr. 29, '62.
2d Lieut. Alex. F. Pope,	Appointed April 24, 1861. captain of artillery March 26, 1864.
2d Lieut. Edw. P. Lumpkin,	Appointed April 24, 1861.
Ensign Pope Barrow,	Appointed April 24, 1861.
Lieut. Columbus W. Motes,	Appointed April 29, 1862.
Lieut. Thomas A. Murray,	Appointed April 29, 1862.
2d Lieut. Henry Jennings,	Appointed April 29, 1862.
2d Lieut. Geo. J. Newton,	Appointed June —, 1862.
2d Lieut. L. C. Cooper,	Appointed Jan. 1, 1864.

WASHINGTON ARTILLERY. Assigned as 1st Independent Georgia Battalion; afterward Company F, 1st Confederate Georgia; afterward Burtwell's and Pritchard's Batteries.

Capt. Isadore P. Girardey,	Appointed April 11, 1861.
Lieut. George T. Barnes,	Appointed April 11, 1861.
Lieut. J. Julius Jacobus,	Appointed April 11, 1861; killed April 7, 1862.
2d Lieut. Charles Spaeth,	Appointed April 11, 1861.
2d Lieut. A. Speliers,	Appointed April —, 1862.

WINGFIELD'S (J. T.) BATTERY. Irwin Artillery. (See Company C, Sumter Battalion.)

WISE GUARDS. Originally Company K, 25th Georgia Infantry; afterward Company B, 22d Battalion Georgia Siege Artillery.

MISCELLANEOUS (GEORGIA ARTILLERY).

Thos. J. Berry, appointed 1st lieutenant of artillery, P. A. C. S., March 16, 1861.

J. A. Alexander, appointed 2d lieutenant of artillery, P. A. C. S., April 17, 1861.

Jno. O. Long, appointed 1st lieutenant of artillery, P. A. C. S., July 1, 1861.

H. Wilkins, appointed 2d lieutenant of artillery, P. A. C. S., December 14, 1861.

Edward C. Anderson, appointed major of artillery, P. A. C. S., May 18, 1861; lieutenant-colonel of artillery, P. A. C. S., May 1, 1862, and colonel of artillery, P. A. C. S., August 1, 1862.

Abner Smead, appointed 1st lieutenant of artillery, P. A. C. S., April 3; 1861, and colonel of artillery, P. A. C. S., August 11, 1862.

S. C. Williams, appointed 1st lieutenant of artillery, P. A. C. S., March 6, 1861, and lieuteant-colonel of artillery, P. A. C. S., April 7, 1864.

Jno. Screven, appointed major of artillery, P. A. C. S., April 17, 1862.

Alfred L. Hartrige, appointed major of artillery, P. A. C. S., April 28, 1863.

W. E. Burnet, appointed major of artillery, P. A. C. S., April 4, 1863.

Geo. W. Anderson, appointed major of artillery, P. A. C. S., April 30, 1863.

L. T. Wofford, appointed major of artillery, P. A. C. S., September 28, 1863.

Robt. A. Stiles, appointed major of artillery, P. A. C. S., January 13, 1865.

Moses H. Wright, appointed 1st lieutenant of artillery, P. A. C. S., July 17, 1861, and captain of artillery, P. A. C. S., June 9, 1862.

Edward N. Thurston, appointed captain of artillery, P. A. C. S., July 31, 1862, and major of artillery, P. A. C. S., March 1, 1865.

Geo. Arnold, appointed captain of artillery, P. A. C. S., October 23, 1862.

S. H. Starr, appointed 1st lieutenant of artillery, P. A.
C. S., March 26, 1864, and captain of artillery, P. A. C. S.,
March 1, 1865.

J. G. Reynolds, appointed 1st lieutenant of artillery,
P. A. C. S., June 4, 1862, and captain of artillery, P. A.
C. S., March 26, 1864.

A. T. Cunningham, appointed 1st lieutenant of artillery, P. A. C. S., May 20, 1862.

W. F. Johnson, appointed 1st lieutenant of artillery,
P. A. C. S., July 5, 1862.

Wm. D. Harden, appointed 1st lieutenant of artillery,
P. A. C. S., July 19, 1862, and captain of artillery, P. A.
C. S., July 13, 1863.

Wm. A. Wright, appointed 1st lieutenant of artillery,
P. A. C. S., August 6, 1862.

H. S. Cunningham, appointed 1st lieutenant of artillery, P. A. C. S., October 6, 1863.

Geo. Howard King, appointed 1st lieutenant of artillery, P. A. C. S., October 6, 1863, and captain of artillery,
P. A. C. S., June 13, 1864.

T. B. Cabaniss, appointed 1st lieutenant of artillery,
P. A. C. S., March 26, 1864.

S. F. Fenney, appointed 1st lieutenant of artillery,
P. A. C. S., March 26, 1864.

C. N. Featherston, appointed 2d lieutenant of artillery,
P. A. C. S., October 6, 1863.

C. Compton, appointed 2d lieutenant of artillery, P. A.
C. S., October 6, 1863.

Thos. G. Barrett, appointed 2d lieutenant of artillery,
P. A. C. S., February 16, 1864.

W. R. Atkinson, appointed 2d lieutenant of artillery,
P. A. C. S., March 8, 1865.

R. F. Wright, appointed 2d lieutenant of artillery,
P. A. C. S., March 8, 1865.

Gordon, E. C., lieut. A. D. C., June 9, 1864.

Grant, Jas. B., lieut. A. D. C., May 6, 1865.

The best estimate that can be made of troops Georgia fur-
nished, first and last, to the Confederate Army is between 120,-
000 and 125,000 men.

GENERAL OFFICERS COMMISSIONED BY THE STATE OF GEORGIA, AND IN STATE SERVICE 1861-1865.

Jackson, Henry Rootes, Major-General, afterwards Brigadier-General in the Provisional Army of the Confederate States; died March 28, 1898.

Smith, Gustavus W., Major-General. Major-General in Provisional Army of Confederate States. Died June 24, 1896.

Walker, W. H. T., Mayor-General of 1st Division of Georgia State Troops, Apr. 25, 1861; afterwards Brigadier-General P. A. C. S.; afterwards Brigadier-General of Georgia State Troops; afterwards Brigadier-General, P. A. C. S.; afterwards Major-General P. A. C. S., killed near Atlanta, July 22, 1864.

Wayne, Henry C., Major-General, Adjutant and Inspector-General of the State of Georgia with rank of Colonel, November 12, 1860. Adjutant and Inspector -General of the State of Georgia with rank of Major-General, November 30, 1861. Brigadier-General, Provisional Army of the Confederate States, December 16, 1861. Declined the appointment. Died March 15, 1883.

Anderson, C. D., Brigadier-General. Died Feb. 23, 1901.

Capers, F. W., Brigadier-General. Died Jan. 12, 1892.

Carswell, R. W., Brigadier-General. Died in 1886.

Harrison, George P. Sr., Brigadier-General. Died in 1907.

McCay, Henry K., Brigadier-General. Died July 30, 1886.

Phillips, P. J., Brigadier-General. Died Oct. 12, 1876.

Phillips, William, Brigadier-General. Died Sept. 25, 1908.

GENERAL OFFICERS OF THE CONFEDERATE ARMY APPOINTED FROM GEORGIA, THEIR COMMANDS, AND STAFF OFFICERS, AS FAR AS ASCERTAINED, AND PREVIOUS SERVICE, IF ANY, IN THE U. S. ARMY.

EDWARD PORTER ALEXANDER.

Cadet U. S. Military Academy July, 1857; brevet lieutenant of engineers July, 1857; resigned May 1, 1861.

Captain Corps of Engineers, C. S. A., April 2, 1861; engineer and chief of signal service on staff of Gen. P. G. T. Beauregard July, 1861, to August, 1861; chief of ordnance, Army of Northern Virginia, August, 1861, to November 8, 1862; lieutenant-colonel of artillery December 31, 1861; colonel of artillery December 5, 1862; commanding Alexander's Battalion of Artillery November 8, 1862, to February 26, 1864; acting chief of artillery, Longstreet's Corps, September 25, 1863, to February 26, 1864; brigadier-general of artillery, P. A. C. S., February 26, 1864; chief of artillery, Longstreet's Corps, Army of Northern Virginia, to surrender at Appomattox.

STAFF.

Colston, Fred M., captain, chief of Ord. Off., May, 1864.

Franklin, J. H., major A. C. S., April 1864.

Haskell, James (Jos.) C., captain A. A. G., March, 1864.

Mason, Willie T., 1st lieutenant, C. S. A., A. D. C., March, 1864.

Middleton, John J., Jr., major A. Q. M., April, 1864.

Post, W. M., surgeon, May, 1864.

Winthrop, Stephen, captain A. I. G., March, 1864.

NOTE.—One of his brothers, James H. Alexander by name, was captain, signal officer, at Fort Caswell, May 26, 1862; chief signal officer to General Beauregard April 8, 1863, and major A. A. G. to Gen. J. F. Gilmer September 14, 1863.

GEORGE THOMAS ANDERSON.

Second lieutenant independent company **Georgia** Mounted Volunteers, U. S. A., May 27, 1847; captain of cavalry, U. S. A., March 1, 1855; resigned June 11, 1858.

Colonel 11th Georgia regiment infantry July 2, 1861; brigadier-general November 1, 1862.

Brigade composed of 7th, 8th, 9th and 11th Georgia, and 1st Kentucky regiments. Afterward the 59th Georgia was substituted for the 1st Kentucky (Hood's), afterward Field's division, Longstreet's Corps, Army of Northern Virginia. Died at Anniston, Ala., April 4; 1901.

STAFF.

Arnold, ..., ... July, 1863.

Daniels, Charles, vol. A. D. C., June, 1862.

Hardwick, Charles C., captain (8th Ga. Inf.), **A. A. G.**, November 8, 1862.

Jackson, T. C., 1st lieutenant A. D. C. (Va. Bat.), November 1, 1862 (vol. A. D. C.).

Tenille, W. A., captain A. I. G. (9th Ga. Reg.), November 19, 1863.

Fouche, Robt. T., lieutenant A. A. D. C., Sept., 1864.

ROBT. H. ANDERSON.

Cadet U. S. Military Academy, July, 1857; second lieutenant 7th infantry July, 1857; second lieutenant 9th infantry December, 1857. Resigned May, 1861.

First lieutenant corps of artillery, C. S. A., March 16, 1861; major, assistant adjutant-general September, 1861; major First Battalion Georgia Sharpshooters June 20, 1862; colonel Fifth Georgia cavalry (temporary rank), 1862; colonel Fifth Georgia cavalry, January 20, 1863; brigadier-general, P. A. C. S., July 26, 1864.

Brigade composed of the Fifth Georgia and the 1st, 3d, 8th and 10th Confederate regiments of cavalry, Kelly's division, Army of Tennessee. Died February 8, 1888.

STAFF.

Allen, J. F., captain A. C. S., ..., 1863.

Footman, R. H., captain A. Q. M., July, 1864.

Gordon, W. W., captain A. I. G. July, 1864, Dec. 15, 1864 (lieut. Ga. Hussars July, 1861; captain A. A. G. Mercer's Brigade Nov., 1861).

Gowan, T. F., captain A. C. S., January, 1863 (5th Ga. cavalry).

McFarland, J. T., surgeon med. dir. July, 1864.

Walthour, W. L., captain A. I. G.; captain Liberty Troops, afterward G. troops, 5th cavalry, 1861.

Yonge, Philip, lieutenant A.D. C., July, 1864 (2d lieutenant 5th cavalry 1863).

Anderson, McKenzie, 1st lieutenant A. D. C.

HENRY LEWIS BENNING.

Colonel Seventeenth Georgia Infantry August, 1861; brigadier-general January 17, 1863.

Brigade composed of the 2d, 15th, 17th and 20th Georgia regiments of infantry, Hood's division, Army of Northern Virginia. Died July 8, 1875.

STAFF.

Alexander, W. T. ,captain A. A. G., 1863.

Ballard, W. S., major A. C. S., March 6, 1863.

Benning, S. J., captain A. A. G. Jan. 17, 1863 to Nov. 4, 1864.

Bird, Wm. Edgeworth, captain A. A. G. 1864; major A. Q. M. Feb., 1863.

DuBose, Dudley M., lieutenant A. D. C. March, 1862· captain A. A. G. ——, 1862.

Hill, R. C., capt. A. A. G., 1863.

Lofton, B. H., sgt. ord. off., 1864.

Moses, R. J., major A. C. S., 1863.

Mott, John R., lieutenant A. D. C., January, 1863.

Perry, Heman H., captain A. I. G., December 31, 1861.

Rains, Thos. A., surgeon, 1862-3.

Tempe, Robert, lieutenant A. D. C. 1862 .

WILLIAM R. BOGGS.

Graduated from U. S. Military Academy at West Point in 1853; 2d lieutenant of ordinance; resigned 1861; captain corps of engineers May, 1861; resigned December 21, 1861; colonel of artillery, July 14, 1862. Brigadier-general November 4, 1862; chief of staff to Gen. E. Kirby Smith; commanding trans-Mississippi Department.

STAFF.

Boggs, Robt., lieutenant A. D. C., December 4, 1862.

WILLIAM M. BROWNE.

Aide-de-camp to President Davis, with rank of colonel of cavalry, 1861; brigadier-general; appointed February 18, 1865, but Senate did not confirm. Died at Athens, Ga., April 28, 1883.

NOTE.—There were, among the members of General Browne's staff, the following: **Patrick Looney,** captain and A. A. G.;

DeSaussure Ford, M. D., surgeon and major; **Albert Sidney A. G.**; **DeSassure Ford, M. D.**, surgeon and major; **Albert Sidney Rodgers,** captain and A. I. G.; **John W. Clark,** 1st lieutenant and A. D. C.; **R. L. Bloomfield,** Q. M. and major, and **R. C. Campbell,** captain and V. A. D. C.

GOODE BRYAN.

Graduated at the U. S. Military Academy at West Point in 1834; second lieutenant U. S. infantry; resigned, 1860.

Colonel 16th Ga. infantry February 15, 1862; brigadier-general August 29, 1863; resigned September 20, 1864.

Brigade composed of the 10th, 50th, 53d and 55th Georgia regiments of infantry, McLaws' division, Longstreet's corps, Army of Northern Virginia. Died August 16, 1885.

STAFF.

Brent, Joseph, —, Lancaster, Md.

Kibbee, C. C., capt. 10th Ga. regiment, A. A. A. G., August, 1864.

Walker, James, captain A. A. G., November 4, 1864.

Walker, Jas. W., captain A. I. G., August, 1864.

Townsend, Jno. H., lieutenant A. D. C., September 9, 1863.

HOWELL COBB.

Colonel 16th Georgia regiment of infantry July 15, 1861; brigadier-general February 13, 1862; major-general September 9, 1863.

Brigade composed of the 15th North Carolina, 2d Louisiana, the 16th and 24th Georgia regiments of infantry, and Cobb's Legion, Army of Northern Virginia; commanding Reserve Forces of the State of Georgia; died in New York City, October 9, 1868.

STAFF.

Barrow, Pope, captain A. D. C., April 22, 1863, July, 1864.

Cobb, Howell, Jr., lieutenant A. D. C., July, 1864.

Cobb, John A., captain A. D. C., April 22, 1862.

Cobb, Lamar, major and A. A. G., July, 1864.

Gwin, William, captain April 2, 1862.

Mallett, R. J., captain A. A. G., July, 1864.

Pope, A. F., captain ord. off. July, 1864.

Thomas, Robert, major, April 22, 1862.

Barrow, Jas., captain A. A. G., March 6, 1862.

Rutherford, Jno. C., captain A. A. G., January 10, 1863.

Hallett, R. J., captain A. A. G., September 23, 1863.

THOMAS R. R. COBB.

Colonel Cobb's Georgia Legion August 28, 1861; brigadier-general November 1, 1862.

Brigade composed of the 16th, 18th and 24th Georgia regiments of infantry, Cobb's Georgia Legion, Phillips' Georgia Legion and 3d battalion Georgia Sharpshooters, McLaws' division, Longstreet's corps, Army of Northern Virginia. Killed at Fredericksburg, Va., December 13, 1862.

NOTE.—It may be mentioned that **John W. Clark,** of Augusta, Ga., held the position of 1st lieutenant and A. D. C. to Gen. T. R. R. Cobb at the time the latter was killed. Other members of General Cobb's staff were **John C. Rutherford,** of Athens, Ga., captain and A. A. G.; **Charles Lumpkin,** lieutenant; **MacPherson Berrien,** of Burke County, Ga.; captain and A. I. G.; and **Rev. R. K. Porter,** captain and chaplain. **Miller G. Lumpkin** was captain and commissary of Cobb's Georgia Legion in 1861. Of that Legion T. R. R. Cobb was then the colonel and Lumpkin may properly be included in his staff. **S. G. White** was its surgeon.

ALFRED HOLT COLQUITT.

Additional paymaster U. S. volunteers June, 1846. Resigned January 31, 1848.

Colonel 6th Georgia regiment of infantry May 27, 1861; brigadier-general September 1, 1862.

Command composed of the 6th, 19th, 23d, 27th and 28th Georgia regiments of infantry, D. H. Hill's division, Army of Northern Virginia. Died at Washington City March 26, 1894.

STAFF.

Colquitt, H. H., lieutenant Vol. A. D. C., May, 1863.

Ely, R. N., major A. Q. M., 1862.

Estill, R. F. (Harry?), lieutenant ord. off. Dec., 1862.

Grattan, G. G., lieutenant A. D. C., October, 1862; captain A. A. G. May, 1863, November 4, 1864.

Jackson, Henry, captain A. A. G., July, 1864.

Jordan, R. P., lieutenant (6th Ga. regt.); A. A. A. G. from May, 1862; killed at Sharpsburg, Sept., 1862.

Mettauer, H. A., surgeon.

Morgan, J. B., major A. A. D. C., 1862.

Randle, J. T., lieutenant A. D. C., May, 1863; killed at Battery Wagner September, 1863.

Borcke, Heros von, maj. A. A. G.

PHILIP COOK.

Served in Captain Black's company in the Seminole war, 1836.

Colonel 4th Georgia regiment of infantry, November 1, 1862; brigadier-general August 5, 1864.

Succeeded Brigadier-general Doles in command of his brigade ,composed of the 4th, 12th, 21st and 44th Georgia regiments of infantry, Rodes' division, Jackson's corps, Army of Northern Virginia; died at Atlanta, Ga., May 22, 1894.

Snead, F. T., captain 'staff A. A. G. November 4, 1864.

Law, Chas. H., lieut. A. D. C., August 5, 1864.

ALFRED CUMMING.

Cadet at U. S. Military Academy July, 1849; brevet 2d lieutenant 8th infantry July 1, 1849; 2d lieutenant 7th infantry July 16, 1850; 1st lieutenant 10th infantry March 3, 1855; captain July 20, 1856; resigned January 19, 1861.

Major corps of infantry, C. S. A., March 16, 1861; lieutenant-colonel 10th Georgia infantry June, 1861; colonel 10th Georgia infantry September 25, 1862; brigadier-general October 29, 1862.

Brigade composed of the 34th, 36th, 39th and 56th Georgia regiments of infantry, Stevenson's division, Army of the West.

STAFF.

Clemons, Welcom G., major asst. quartermaster, October 29, 1862.

Evans, H., major A. D. C., May-July, 1863.

Lamar, De Rosset, captain A. D. C., 1863-4.

Mayo, J. H. F., major A. C. S., October 29, Nov. 13, 1862.

Phinizy, Charles H., capt. A. A. G. Oct. 29, 1862.

NOTE.—At the time of reorganization of Gen. J. E. Johnston's army near the end of the War, there was a rumor afloat among the soldiers to the effect that Captain Phinizy was to be promoted to colonelcy of 39th Georgia Infantry. The rumor, however, eventuated in nothing material, though it is unofficially believed that specified appointment was made before the fall of the Confederacy.

Smith, E. R., captain A. I. G., Nov. 10, 1862; captain May-July, 1863.

Steiner, Frank, lieutenant A. D. C. October 29, 1862, November 7, 1862.

Wise, George D., lieutenant May-July, 1863; captain ord. off. Sept. 18, 1863.

Banner, M. R., lieutenant, ord., November 3, 1864.

Bass, J. W., lieutenant A. A. I. G., November 4, 1864.

Cody, Adolphus, A. A. I. G., November, 1863.

GEORGE DOLES.

Colonel 4th Georgia regiment of infantry May 8, 1861; brigadier-general November 1, 1862.

Brigade composed of the 4th, 12th, 21st and 44th Georgia regiments of infantry, D. H. Hill's division, Army of Northern Virginia; killed at Bethesda Church, Va., May 30, 1864.

STAFF.

Hawkins, E. A., lieutenant A. D. C., May, 1863.
Furlow, C. T., ——, July, 1863.
Jones, Richard V., lieutenant A. I. G., May ——, 1863.
Snead, F. T., captain A. A. G., May-July, 1863.

DUDLEY McIVER DuBOSE.

Colonel 15th Georgia regiment of infantry January, 1863; brigadier-general November 16, 1864.

Brigade composed of the 18th, 16th and 24th Georgia regiments of infantry, Cobb's and Phillips' Legions, and the 3d battalion Georgia Sharpshooters, Kershaw's division, Longstreet's corps, Army of Northern Virginia; died, March 4, 1883.

STAFF.

Bird, S. M., major A. Q. M., 1864-'65.
Crane, Benj. E., major A. C. S. (1864-'65).
Hackett, T. H., captain A. I. G., 1864-'65.
Pierce, Geo. F., Jr., captain A. A. A. G., 1864-'65.

CLEMENT A. EVANS.

Major 31st Georgia infantry November 19, 1861; colonel 31st Georgia regiment infantry May 13, 1862; brigadier-general May 19, 1864.

Brigade composed of the 13th, 26th, 31st, 38th, 60th and 61st Georgia regiments of infantry. Subsequently the 12th Georgia regiment was added to the brigade. Army Northern Virginia.

STAFF.

Cooper, George F., brigade surgeon, December, 1862.
Hall, Edward, captain A. A. G., November, 1864.
Lawton, E. P., captain A. A. G., Dec., 1862.
Gordon, E. C., lieutenant A. D. C., June 9, 1864.
Reid, Francis W., major A. C. S., June 12, 1862.

WILLIAM MONTGOMERY GARDNER.

Cadet U. S. Military Academy, July, 1846; brevet 2d lieutenant 1st infantry July, 1846; 2d lieutenant 7th infantry February 16, 1847; transferred to 2d infantry

July, 1847; 1st lieutenant October 16, 1849; captain March 3, 1855; brevet 1st lieutenant August 20, 1847, for gallant and meritorious conduct in the battles of Contreras and Churubusco, Mexico; resigned January 19, 1861.

Major corps of infantry C. S. A., March 16, 1861; colonel 8th Georgia regiment of infantry July 21, 1861; brigadier-general November 14, 1861.

Commanding paroled prisoners at Demopolis, Ala., 1863; commanding military prisons in States east of the Mississippi river excluding Georgia and Alabama, 1864; commanding local defense troops, Department of Richmond, September, 1864; commanding at Salisbury, N. C., November, 1864; commanding post at Richmond, Va., January, 1865; on duty with Gen. Howell Cobb commanding District of Georgia, March, 1865; died at Memphis, Tenn., June 16, 1904.

STAFF.

Barth, William G., captain A. A. G., March 20, 1865.
Lanier, John S., ——.
White, J. H., surgeon, chief surgeon, March 20, 1865.
Winder, R. B., major, chief quartermaster, March 20, 1865.
Grant, Jas. B., lieutenant A. D. C., May 6, 1865.
Rose, Alex., lieutenant A. D. C., December 2, 1862.

LUCIUS J. GARTRELL.

Colonel 7th Georgia infantry March 31, 1861; resigned December ——, 1862, having been elected to the Confederate Congress; brigadier-general August 22, 1864.

Commanding 2d brigade of Georgia Reserves, composed of the 1st, 2d, 3d and 4th regiments; died at Atlanta, Ga., April 7, 1891.

STAFF.

Hill, Miles H., captain A. G., 1863.
Nichols, William M., lieutenant A. A. G., 1863.
Irwin, Robt. C., lieutenant A. D. C., November 14, 1864.

VICTOR J. B. GIRARDEY.

Brigadier-general, July 30, 1864.

Commanding Brigadier-general Wright's brigade, composed of the 3d, 22d, 40th and 48th Georgia regiments of infantry, and 2d Georgia battalion of infantry, Anderson's division, A. P. Hill's corps, Army of Northern Virginia.

Killed at Petersburg, Va., August, 1864.

STAFF.

Evans, J. K., captain A. A. A. G. 1864 (previously lieutenant in 48th Georgia).

Hughes, H. S., captain, brig. com'y sub., 1862. (Previously captain "Lawson's Greys," 3d Ga.)

McWhorter, R. L., major, brigadier Q. M. 1862. (Previously in 3d Ga.)

Swinney, W. M. (M. E.?), chief brigade surgeon, 1862. (Previously surgeon of 48th Georgia.)

JOHN BROWN GORDON.

Appointed from Alabama, lieutenant-colonel 6th Alabama Regiment Infantry, Dec. 26, 1861; colonel 6th Alabama Regiment Infantry, April 28, 1862; brigadier-general, P. A. C. S., May 7, 1863; major-general, P. A. C. S., May 14, 1864. There is no evidence in the official records that he was ever promoted to grade of lieutenant-general, P. A. C. S., or that he ever received his commission as such. All claims awarding him this rank are, therefore, unofficial, and cannot be sustained by the records on file at the war department, Washington, D. C. At the Appomattox surrender he signed simply "J. B. Gordon, major-general, commanding corps."

Brigade composed of the 13th, 26th, 31st, 38th, 60th and 61st Georgia regiments of infantry (originally, Lawton's Brigade); the 6th and 12th Georgia Battalions of Infantry, Early's Division, Army of Northern Virginia.

Division composed of the Brigades of Evans, Terry and York, Army of Northern Virginia. Commanding 2d Corps, Army of Northern Virginia, as major-general; commanding left wing Army of Northern Virginia, May, 1865.

STAFF.

Douglas, H. Kyd., major A. A. G., Nov. 4, 1864.

Halsey, Don P., captain A. A. G., 1862.

Jones, Thos. G., lieutenant A. D. C., Jan. 2, 1863, and April 4, 1865.

Moore, Edwin L., major A. A. G., November 4, 1864.

Stephens, J. H., senior surgeon, July, 1864.

Wilmer, S. K., lieutenant signal officer, July —, 1864.

Hunter, Robert W., major A. A. G.

Pace, James M., captain A. A. G., Nov. 27, 1862, to April 9, 1865.

Ballard, W. S., major C. S., Jan. 5, 1864.

Graves, J. T., captain A. C. S., August 8, 1863.

Myers, Wm. B, major A. A. G., April 8, 1865.

WILLIAM J. HARDEE.

Cadet U. S. Military Academy, July, 1838; 1st lieutenant of dragoons, December 3, 1839; captain of dragoons, September 18, 1844; brevetted major and lieutenant-colonel for gallantry in Mexican War (1847); a little later, promoted to major of 2d U. S. Cavalry; commandant of cadets, U. S. Military Academy, 1856-'60; resigned January 31, 1861.

Colonel corps of cavalry, C. S. A., March 16, 1861; brigadier-general June 17, 1861; major-general October 7, 1861; lieutenant-general October 10, 1862.

Brigade (1861) composed of 1st, 2d, 5th, 6th, 7th and 8th Arkansas regiments of infantry; commanding division under Gen. A. S. Johnston in Kentucky and Tennessee, 1861-2; commanding Fort Morgan, Mobile Bay, 1861; commanding 3d corps, Army of the Mississippi, composed of Hindman's, Wood's and Cleburne's divisions; commanding Army of the Mississippi, afterwards called Army of Tennessee, 1862; commanding left wing of Gen. Bragg's army in Kentucky campaign, composed of Buckner's and Patton Anderson's divisions and Wheeler's cavalry; commanding army corps consisting of Breckenridge's and Cleburne's divisions; commanding right wing of Army of Tennessee, consisting of Cheatham's, Stevenson's and Walker's divisions; commanding Army of Tennessee December, 1863; commanding army corps consisting of Cheatham's, Cleburne's, Walker's and Bate's divisions, May to September, 1864; commanding Department of South Carolina, Georgia and Florida, October, 1864; commanding troops at Bentonville, N. C., March, 1865. Died at Wytheville, Va., November 6, 1873. 1873.

STAFF.

Bailey, James, mil. storekeeper at Greenville, Mo., August 11, 1861; A. Q. M. Hindman's legion, A. A. Q. M., August, 1861.

Black, Samuel L., lieutenant A. I. G., July 5, 1862; captain A. I. G. January 1, 1863; lieutenant-colonel July-October, 1863.

Blake, E. D., lieutenant-colonel, inspector-general, July 5, 1862.

Boutwell, ——., lieutenant A. D. C., April 6, 7, 1862.

Breysacher, A. L., surgeon medical inspector July 5, 1862—July, 1863.

Bridewell, L. O., major chief quartermaster, April 6, 7, 1862.

Buntwell, ——, lieutenant A. A. D. C., April 6, 7, 1862.

Chambliss, Nathaniel R., captain chief ordnance, Dec. 5, 1861.

Claiborne, Thos., captain vol. A. D. C., January 1, 1863.

Clare, William, captain A. A. D. C., April 6, 7, 1862.

Clarkson, A. W., captain A. A. D. C., April 6, 7, 1862.

Flash, Henry L., captain volunteer A. D. C., July 5, 1862.

Gassett, C. W., major chief quartermaster, January 1, 1863.

Gonzales, A. J., colonel, chief of artillery, Dec. 30, 1864.

Govan, Wm. H., captain A. Q. M., August 11, 1861.

Green, J. W., captain, engineer's off., Dec., 1862.

Hanauer, Lewis, colonel A. Q. M., purch. agt. July 23, 1861.

Hardee, T. L., lieutenant A. D. C., April 25, 1862.

Hardee, T. S., captain A. D. C., July 5, 1862.

Harrison, Thomas, captain A. A. D. C ., June 2, 1864.

Hay, E. B., A. A. G., January 16, 1865.

Hoxton, Llewellen, major C. A., December, 1862.

Hunt, T. W., lieutenant acting A. D. C., April 6, 7, 1862; captain A. I. G. January 1, 1863, July 25, 1863.

Johnson, John M., surgeon medical director, July 25, 1863.

Jones, ——, colonel, March, 1863.

Kearney, William, lieutenant A. I. G., April 6, 7, 1862.

Kennard, J. M., major, chief ordnance January 1, July 25, 1863.

Kennard, P. T., volunteer A. D. C., August 9, 1861.

Lanford, R. C., major A. C. S., Feb. 24, 1862; April 1, 1864.

Beatty, ——, Judge Advocate, February 13, 1863.

Lay, Jno. F., major A. A. I. G., March 29, 1865.

Burtwell, J. R. B., lieut. A. A. D. C., April 6, 1862.

Gholson, Samuel J., Col. Judge Advocate, Feb. 13, 1863.

Lawrence, G. W., surgeon medical director, April 6, 7, 1862.

Lawrentree, August, lieutenant (Hindman's Legion).

Liddell, St. John R., colonel volunteer A. D. C., acting ordn. officer, July 22, 1861.

McMicken, C. G., lieutenant chief signal officer, Jan. 6, 1865.

Marmaduke, Jno. S., lieutenant A. D. C. and A. A. G., August 7, 1861.

Mason, Richard M., chief A. Q. M., relieved July 12, 1864.

Memminger, C. G., chief signal officer, Jan. 11, 1865.

Moore, John C., judge advocate, July 5, 1862.

Moore, W. E., captain com'y., July, 1861.

Patton, Montrose A., surgeon general medical director, District of Arkansas, August 23, 1861.

Patton, Yandell S., major chief Q. M., 1864.

Pearre, Aubrey, captain acting ordn. officer Hardee's corps, 1864-5.

Perkins, Hardin, colonel volunteer A. D. C., Dec. 5, 1861.

Perkins, S. H., colonel volunteer A. D. C., Aug. 9, 1861, July, 1862.

Pickett, W. D., major A. A. G. and chief of staff April 6, 7, 1862; colonel A. I. G., Jan. 28, 1865.

Poole, D. H., lieutenant A. A. A. G., July 5, 1862; captain A. A. G., Jan. 1, 1863; major A. I. G., Aug. 20, 1863.

Poole, W. G., captain 1st Florida regiment A. A. G., June 2, 1864.

Pope, John, captain chief Q. M., Dec. 5, 1861.

Presstman, S. W., captain eng. off, Dec. 30, 1862.

Riley, E. B. D., major ord. offi., May 19, 1863.

Roy, T. B., captain A. A. G., July 5, 1862; A. A. G. chief of staff July 25, 1863; A. A. G. Jan. 5, 1865.

Shoup, F. A., 1st lieutenant C. S. A., A. D. C. and A. A. A. G. July 23, 1861; major C. A. April 6, 7, 1862.

Thomas, J. G., acting medical director, April 5, 1865.

White, D. G., lieutenant A. A. G., April 16, lieutenant inspector artillery, July, 1861; major A. A. G. Jan.-July, 1863.

Whitehead, ——, captain, March, 1865.

Whitthorne, W. C., adjutant general of Tennessee, vol. A. D. C. Jan. 1, 1863.

Wicks, Moses J., major chief com'y, July 5, 1862.

Wilkins, W. W., lieutenant A. I. G. (?), July 5, 1862.

Wilson, ——, lieutenant A. A. D. C., April 6, 7, 1862.

Yandell, D. W., surgeon medical director, July 5, 1862, Jan. 1, 1863.

GEORGE PAUL HARRISON, JR.

Appointed from Georgia. A Colonel commanding a Brigade, composed of 1st Georgia Regulars, 32d, 47th and 5th Regiments, Georgia Volunteers, and 5th Regiment of Georgia Reserves.

Blount, George M., 1st lieutenant A. A. A. G., Feb. 20, 1864.

Cohen, Gratz, captain A. D. C.

Guerard, E. L., captain A. Q. M.

Hundley, Wm. B., major A. I. G.

Moreno, S. A., captain A. A. G., March, 1865.

NOTE.—**Colonel Robert Johnson Henderson,** of 42d Georgia Infantry, was a colonel commanding a brigade. Died February 3, 1891.

Crews, Charles C., a colonel (of 2d Georgia Cavalry) commanding a brigade under Major-General Joseph Wheeler, composed of 1st, 2d, 3d, 4th and 6th Regiments, Georgia Cavalry, Army of Tennessee. He came, as we understand, from Southwest Georgia. Date of death unknown.

It may be metnioned that **Major-General John Stevens Bowen,** P. A. C. S., of Missouri, was a native of Savannah, Ga., he becoming a citizen of his adopted State in 1857. He was promoted to grade of brigaier-general, P. A. C. S., in 1862, and to that of major-general, P. A. C. S., in 1863. Died July 16, 1863.

It should be mentioned that **Edward Dorr Tracy,** of Alabama, a native Georgian, was promoted to grade of brigadier-general, P. A. C. S., in 1862, his brigade consisting of the 20th, 23d, 30th, 31st and 46th lAabama regiments of infantry, Stevenson's Division, Army of Tennessee. Died near Port Gibson, Miss., May 1, 1863.

ALFRED IVERSON.

Second Lieutenant Seymour's battalion Georgia Volunteers in Mexican War, August, 1847; honorably mustered out July 11, 1848; 1st lieutenant 1st cavalry March, 1855; resigned March 21, 1861.

Captain corps of infantry, C. S. A., March 16, 1861; colonel 29th North Carolina Infantry August 20, 1861; brigadier general November 1, 1862.

Commanding brigade, composed of the 5th, 12th, 20th and 23rd North Carolina regiments of infantry, D. H. Hill's division, Jackson's corps, Army of Northern Virginia. In 1864 brigade composed of the 1st, 2d, 3d, 4th and 6th Georgia regiments of cavalry, Martin's division, Wheeler's corps, Army of Tennessee.

General Iverson was appointed from North Carolina, but he commanded Georgia troops.

STAFF.

Coleman, H. E., lieutenant-colonel volunteer A. D. C., June, 1863.

Ector, J. T., lieutenant A. D. C., June, 1863.

Halsey, D. P., captain A. A. G., May, 1863.

Garland, ——, major A. C. S., 1863.

Payne, ——, major A. C. S., 1863.
Woods, J. J., captain A. I. G., 1863.
Branham, Isham R., capt. A. A. G., October 24, 1863.

HENRY ROOTES JACKSON.

Brigadier-general June 4, 1861; resigned December 2, 1861; reappointed brigadier-general September 21, 1863.

Brigade composed of the 1st Confederate, the 25th, 29th, 30th and 66th Georgia regiments of infantry, and a battalion of infantry. In May, 1862, composed of the 3d Arkansas, 31st Virginia, and 1st and 12th Georgia regiments of infantry, and a battalion of Georgia infantry. July 14, 1861, assumed command of the Army of the Northwest. October 3, 1861, commanding a division in the Army of the Northwest.

Died at Savannah, Ga., May 23, 1898.

STAFF.

Andrews, Garnett, 2nd lieutenant A. A. G., Aug. 5, 1861.

Barton, S. M., lieutenant-colonel 3d Arkansas regiment; A. A. G. Oct. 21, 1861.

Bloom, F. S., major A. D. C. Oct. 7, 1861.

Humphries, W. D., lieutenant A. D. C. Aug. 3, 1861.

Jackson, Henry, cadet, A. D. C. Oct. 7, 1861.

Garnett, Andrew, lieutenant A. A. A. G., August 3, 1861.

JOHN KING JACKSON.

Colonel 5th Georgia Infantry, 1861. Brig. Gen. Jan. 14, 1862.

Brigade composed of the 5th and 8th Mississippi, the 5th Georgia and 1st Confederate regiments of infantry, the 2d Battalion Georgia Sharpshooters, and a battery of light artillery. Subsequently commanding the 3d brigade in Reserve corps, Army of the Mississippi, composed of the 17th, 18th, 21st and 24th Alabama and 5th Georgia regiments of infantry, and Burtwell's light battery of artillery, Army of Tennessee. August to September 29, 1864, commanding District of Florida, in Department of South Carolina, Georgia and Florida.

Died at Milledgeville, Ga., Feb. 27, 1866.

STAFF.

Barrett, Thomas G., ordn. officer captain volunteer A. D. C., Jan. 1, 1863.

Beauchamp, J. J., major A. C. S. Feb. 28, 1863.

Bryan, A. M., captain inspector-general Oct. 19, 1862.

Catho (?), R. S., captain prov. mar. Chattanooga, Tenn., March 5, 1863.

Cheatham, R. S., A. A. G. April 7-Feb. 23, 1863.

Cumming, Joseph B., captain A. A. G., July 4, 1862; major Jan. 1, 1863.

Note.—Captain A. A. G., Army of Tennessee, October 28, 1864; major (in charge of courtmartial) A. A. G. to Gen. J. E. Johnston, 1865.

Floyd, W. D. C., major A. A. I. G., July 24, 1862; ordnance officer July 28, 1862.

Harris, Samuel, 2nd lieutenant A. A. I. G. July 24, 1862.

Hundley, ——, captain pro. mar. Chattanooga, 1863.

Hunt, S. P., chief surgeon July 24, 1862; surgeon acting inspector hospitals, District Tennessee, Jan., 1863; chief surgeon Oct. 19, 1862.

Jackson, A. M., lieutenant A. D. C. April 1, 1862, Jan. 1, 1863.

Jennison, Geo. A., A. A. A. G., Sept. 24, 1862.

Jones, B. F., A. Q. M. Bridgeport, Ala., Feb. 28, 1863.

King, Hugh M., chief Q. M. July 25, 1862.

Lloyd, W. D. C., major ordnance officer; A. I. G. Feb., 1863.

Moreno, Stephen A., captain A. A. A. G. July 24, 1862; major A. A. G. Nov. 14, 1863.

Montgomery, H. B. T., captain A. C. S. Bridgeport, Ala., March 4, 1863.

Nelms, L. A., A. A. A. G. June, 1861.

Oglesby, Wm. M., A. A. A. G. May 10, 1863.

Pinckney, R. J., captain A. Q. M. acting division Q. M. ——. Relieved July 25, 1862.

Prince, J. L., captain A. Q. M., Bridgeport, Ala., March 4, 1863.

Robertson, F. H., captain acting chief artillery Oct. 28, 1862.

Sanchez, B. S., lieutenant A. D. C. Jan., 1862.

Sibley, W. C., captain division com'y, July 28, 1862.

Stanford, ——, captain assistant division com'y., Oct. 19, 1862.

Thomas, John W., A. A. A. G. May 9, 1863.

Goldthwaite, Henry, major A. A. G., August, 1864.

McKinney, ——, captain ——, November, 1863.

DAVID RUMPLE JONES.

Cadet U. S. Military Academy July, 1846; brevet 2d lieutenant 2d infantry July, 1846; 2d lieutenant Nov.

23, 1846; regimental adjutant April 15, 1847, to December 29, 1848; 1st lieutenant May 7, 1849, to March 3, 1855; brevet captain A. A. G. March 16, 1853; brevet 1st lieutenant August 20, 1847, for gallant and meritorious conduct in battles of Contreras and Churubusco, Mexico. Resigned February 15, 1861.

Major assistant adjutant-general and chief of staff to Gen. G. T. Beauregard April 11, 1861; brigadier-general June 17, 1861; major-general October 11, 1862.

Brigade composed of the 4th, 5th, 6th and 9th South Carolina regiments of infantry, being the 3d brigade, 1st corps, Army of the Potomac; afterwards division composed of the brigades of Toombs, Anderson, Drayton, Kemper, Garnett and Jenkins, Longstreet's corps, Army of Northern Virginia.

Died at Richmond, Va., January 19, 1863.

STAFF.

Adams, Joseph M., major, Q. M.

Barksdale, ——, surgeon, June-Dec., 1862.

Campbell, ——, lieutenant engineer officer June, 1862.

Carell, J. R., captain ——, July, 1861.

Coward, A., captain —— July, 1861; major A. A. G. Dec., 1861.

De L'Aigle, L., captain A. Q. M. June, 1862.

Elford, T. J., major C. S., August, 1861.

Ford, W. J., captain, July, 1861; A. D. C., A. A. Q. M., Dec., 1862.

Haskell, ——, major A. C. S. June, 1862.

Jones, Philip B., Jr., captain volunteer A. D. C. June-Dec., 1862.

Latham, F. G., lieutenant A. A. A. G. July, 1861.

Latrobe, Osman, captain A. & I. G. June-Dec., 1862.

McLemore, O. K., lieutenant A. A. A. G., July, 1861.

Moses, R. J., major A. C. S. Dec., 1862.

Moore, Samuel J. C., captain A. A. G. April, 1863.

Rose, Hugh, volunteer A. D. C. Dec., 1862.

Taylor, E., captain July, 1861.

Thurston, E. N., captain volunteer A. D. C. June, 1862; ordnance officer Dec., 1862.

Williams, C. W., volunteer A. D. C. Dec., 1862.

Young, H. E., captain A. A. G. Dec., 1862.

Garnett, Jno. J., major C. A., June, 1862.

Jones, Samuel P., lieutenant A. D. C., October 27, 1862.

NOTE.—Another addition to above list may be made in the person of **Col. Wm. H. King,** of 18th Texas Infantry, a native Georgian, who was assigned to duty by Gen. E. Kirby Smith, of Trans-Mississippi Department, in July, 1864 (?), as brigadier-general, P. A. C. S. He was not, as the records clearly show, appointed by President Davis, or confirmed by the Confederate Senate, as the other Georgia generals were.

ALEXANDER ROBERT LAWTON.

Cadet U. S. Military Academy, July 1, 1839; 2d lieutenant 1st artillery July, 1839; resigned December 31, 1840.

Brigadier-general, P. A. C. S., April 13, 1861; quartermaster-general August 10, 1863.

Brigade composed of the 13th, 26th, 31st, 38th, 60th and 61st Georgia regiments of infantry, Ewell's division, Jackson's corps, Army of Northern Virginia; commanding Ewell's division; commanding Department of Georgia, October 26, 1861; commanding District of Georgia, in Department of South Carolina, Georgia and Florida, May 28, 1862; commanding military district of Savannah, 1861. Died at Clifton Springs, N. Y., July 2, 1896.

STAFF.

Berry, Thomas J., A. D. C. & A. A. A. G. Oct. 25-30, 1861.

Beverly, W. W., lieutenant C. S. infantry, A. A. D. C. December 10, 1861.

Bernan, James H., A. Q. M. April 13, 1861.

Cheves, Edward, A. D. C. 1862. Killed at battle of Cold Harbor June 27, 1862.

Cumming, Montgomery, A. D. C. and A. A. A. G., July 15, 1861.

Echols, William H., captain engineers April 16, 1861.

Elliott, Robt. W. B., lieutenant A. D. C., Oct. 4, 1861.

Gills, G. W., chief of ordnance, April 15, 1861.

Gardner, W. M., major C. S. A., A. A. A. G., May 30, 1861.

Gibbons, Wm. H., major Q. M, 1862.

Hull, Edward W., captain inspector-general, 1862.

Ingraham, H. L., lieutenant ordnance officer Oct., 1862.

Jackson, Henry, cadet A. D. C. July 1, 1862; 2d lieutenant artillery on staff of Gen. W. H. T. Walker, Jan., 1863; ordnance officer to Lucas' battalion artillery, May, 1863; captain A. A. G. on staff of Gen. H. R. Jackson, July, 1863; on staff of A. H. Colquitt, June, July, 1864.

Lawton, Edward P., captain A. A. G. October 1, 1861.

Killed at battle of Fredericksburg, Dec. 13, 1862.

McLaws, L., major, C. S. A., A. A. A. G. May 31, 1861; Q. M. & A. C. S., April 17, 1862.

Reid, F. W., major C. S., 1861.

Richardson, F. H., captain I. G., 1862.

Rockwell, Wm. S., lieutenant-colonel 1st Ga. volunteers, A. A. A. G., July 20, 1861.

Smith, S. J., A. Q. M., July 15, 1861.

Smith, W. D., major 1st Ga. regiment., A. A. A. G., June 25, 1861.

Speer, Daniel N., captain Q. M., 1862.

Stewart, James T., captain A. Q. M., 1861-2.

Wayne, Henry C., colonel adjutant-general; announced as chief of staff to General Lawton, April 17, 1861.

Elliott, Robt., captain A. A. G., October 20, 1863.

Reveley, W. W., lieutenant A. A. D. C., Dec. 10, 1861.

LAFAYETTE McLAWS.

Cadet U. S. Military Academy, July, 1842; brevet 2d lieutenant 6th infantry July 1, 1842; 2d lieutenant 2d infantry, March 16, 1844; 1st lieutenant, February 16, 1847; captain, August 24, 1851; resigned March 23, 1861.

Major corps of infantry, C. S. A., March 10, 1861; colonel 10th Georgia infantry June 17, 1861; brigadier-general September 25, 1861; major-general May 23, 1862.

Brigade in October, 1861, composed of the 15th and 32d Virginia, 10th Louisiana, and the 10th, 53d, and 57th Georgia regiments of infantry, and Manley's light battery of artillery; division in June, 1862, composed of the brigades of Kershaw, Wofford, Humphreys and Bryan; division May 3, 1863, (Chancellorsville) composed of brigades of Wofford, Kershaw, Barksdale and Semmes; in 1864 commanding District of Georgia; in December, 1864, commanding division under General Hardee; in 1865 commanding division under General Hardee, in Gen. J. E. Johnston's army; April 10, 1865, commanding military District of Georgia, by special order of General J. E. Johnston. Died at Savannah, Ga., July 22, 1897.

STAFF.

Atkinson, ——, captain volunteer A. D. C., May —, 1862.

Brown, N. B., captain Dec. 12, 1864; chief Q. M. February 10, 1865.

Cabell, Henry C., colonel C. A., Oct.-Dec., 1862.

Campbell, —., lieutenant engineering officer, Oct.-Dec., 1862.

Costin, E. L., major A. D. C., Oct., 1862; major A. I. G. Dec., 1862.

Cumming, W. H , major, chief surgeon, medical director, Feb. 10, 1865.

Edwards, A. L., lieutenant ordnance officer, Oct.-Dec., 1862.

Edwards, J. F., major A. C. S., Oct.-Dec., 1862; chief C. S. of division Dec., 1862; promoted chief C. S. of corps.

Elliott, R. W. B., captain A. A. G. Dec. 12, 1864.

Fishburne, B. C., major surgeon, medical director, April 10, 1865.

Gilmore, John T., surgeon, medical director, Oct.-Dec., 1862.

Goggin, James M., major A. A. G., April 30, 1862; major A. C. S. Oct., 1862; major A. A. G. Dec., 1862.

Henley, ——, captain volunteer A. D. C., May, 1862.

Huguenin, A., lieutenant A. D. C., Dec. 12, 1864; A. D. C. Feb. 10, 1865.

King, Henry Lord Page, captain A. D. C. ——, 1861; A. D. C., May, 1862, Oct., 1862. Killed at the battle of Fredericksburg, Dec., 1862. Still serving as such when killed.

King, Mallory Page, captain A. A. G. and A. I. G., Dec. 12, 1864; lieutenant-colonel A. I. G. Feb. 10, 1865.

Lamar, G. B., lieutenant A. D. C. and A. A. A. G., Dec. 12, 1864; A. D. C. and A. A. A. G., Feb. 10, 1865.

McIntosh, Thomas S., major A. A. G., 1861; captain A. A. G., Oct. 19, 1861; major A. A. G., May, 1862. Killed

Patton, John A., chief surgical division Dec. 12, 1864.

Middleton, Jno. J., Jr., major div. Q. M., Nov. 15, 1863. at Sharpsburg, Sept. 17, 1862.

McLaws, A. H., major Q. M. division, Dec., 1862.

Maxwell, J. A., captain acting chief artillery and ordnance Dec. 12, 1864.

Napier, LeRoy, A. A. D. C. —, 1861.

Patterson, F. W., surgeon July 1, 1863.

Peck, W. D., major A. Q. M., Dec. 13, 1863.

Read, John P. W., captain, chief artillery, May, 1862.

Robertson, J. R., major chief C. S. (at Savannah), April 10, 1863.

Smith, L. Jacquelin, captain, ordnance officer, Feb. 10, 1865.

Taliaferro, E., captain, ordnance officer, Feb. 10, 1865.

Taylor, Henry, captain A. A. D. C. —, 1861, Dec., 1863.

Thomas, J. G., chief surgeon division, April, 1865.

Tucker, Tom S. B., lieutenant A. D. C., April 30, Dec., 1862.

HUGH WEEDON MERCER.

Cadet U. S. Military Academy, July, 1828; brevet 2d lieutenant of artillery and 2d·lieutenant of artillery July 1, 1828; 1st lieutenant October 10, 1835; resigned April 30, 1836.

Colonel 1st Georgia regiment of infantry —, 1861; brigadier-general October 29, 1861.

Brigade composed of the 1st, 54th, 57th and 63d Georgia infantry, Army of Tennessee, commanding at Savannah, Ga.

Died, June 9, 1877.

STAFF.

Anderson, Edward C., Jr., lieutenant A. D. C., Nov. 16, 1861; major cavalry, 1862; colonel 7th Georgia cav., 1863.

Drummond, Edward W., captain, assistant commander 1st Georgia volunteers.

Gordon, William W. (lieutenant Jeff Davis Legion), captain A. A. G., acting inspector, January 11, 1863.

Habersham, Jos. Clay, lieutenant A. D. C., Nov. 16, 1861.

Harden, William D., lieutenant ordnance officer, Dec. 30, 1861; promoted captain and ordnance officer.

Hartridge, A. S. (L.?), lieutenant A. D. C., July 9, 1862; major com'y, 1863.

Mercer, George A., captain A. A. G., Nov. 16, 1861; June, 1862; March, 1863.

Stewart, James T., captain A. Q. M., November 16, 1861; major and Q. M., 1863.

Stoddard, John J., lieutenant A. D. C., May 30, 1863.

Thomas, R. B., lieutenan tartillery corps, C. A., December 10, 1861.

Williams, James S., major, inspector-general, 1864.

PAUL J. SEMMES.

Colonel 2d Georgia regiment of infantry, May 7, 1861; brigadier-general, March 11, 1862.

Brigade composed of the 10th, 50th, 51st and 53d Georgia infantry, McLaws' division, Longstreet's corps, A. N. Va.

Mortally wounded at Gettysburg. Died July 10, 1863.

STAFF.

Briggs, —, captain A. D. C., June and Sept., 1862.

Briggs, E. B., lieutenant A. D. C., April, 1862.

Clemons, Welcom G., captain A. A. G., June, 1862.

Cody, B. H., lieutenant volunteer A. D. C., June and September, 1862.

Costin, E. L., captain A. D. C., June, 1862.

Ellis, R., captain A. A. G., April, 1863.

Gilmore, ——, surgeon, June, 1862.

Redd, ——, lieutenant volunteer A. D. C., June and September, 1862.

JAMES P. SIMMS.

Major 53d Georgia regiment of infantry; colonel 53d Georgia regiment of infantry; brigadier-general Dec. 8, 1864.

Brigade composed of the 10th, 50th, 51st and 52d Georgia regiments of infantry, Kershaw's division, Longstreet's corps, Army of Northern Virginia. Died May 30, 1887.

STAFF.

Kibbee, C. C., captain A. A. A. G., December, 1864.

WILLIAM DUNCAN SMITH.

Cadet U. S. Military Academy, July, 1846; brevet 2d lieutenant 2d dragoons, July, 1846; 2d lieutenant, August, 1847; 1st lieutenant, August 8, 1851; captain, June 4, 1858; resigned January 28, 1861.

Captain corps of cavalry, C. S. A., March 16, 1861; colonel 20th Georgia regiment infantry, July 14, 1861; brigadier-general, March 7, 1862.

Commanding First Military District of South Carolina, in the Department of South Carolina, Georgia and Florida, July 8, 1862; commanding troops on James Island, 1862. Died at Charleston, S. C., October 4, 1862.

STAFF.

King, Mallory Page, captain A. A. G., April 23, 1862.

Habersham, Jos. C., lieutenant A. D. C., April 22, 1862.

G. MOXLEY SORREL.

Captain A. A. G., Longstreet's brigade, September 1, 1861; major A. A. G., Longstreet's division, July 24, 1862; lieutenant-colonel A. A. G., Longstreet's corps, June 23, 1863; brigadier-general, October 31, 1864.

Brigade composed of the 2d, 22d, 48th and 64th Georgia regiments of infantry, and the 2d and 10th Georgia battalions of infantry, Mahone's division, A. P. Hill's corps, A. N. Va.

Died near Roanoke, Va., August 10, 1901.

Hughes, Sidney, major com'y.

McWhorter, W. H., major Q. M., ——.

Perry, Heman H., captain A. A. G., Novemmber, 1864.

Spencer, ——, lieutenant A. D. C., November, 1864.

ISAAC M. St. JOHN.

Captain corps of engineers, C. S. A., February 15, 1862; major of artillery and superintendent of Nitre and Mining corps, April 18, 1862; lieutenant-colonel Nitre and Mining corps, May 28, 1863; brigadier-general and commissary-general, C. S. A., February 16, 1865. Died April 7, 1880.

STAFF.

French, S. B., major A. C. S., 1865.

Noland, B. P., major A. C. S., 1865.

Williams, T. G., colonel A. C. S., 1865.

MARCELLUS A. STOVALL.

Lieutenant-colonel 3d Georgia battalion, October 8, 1861; brigadier-general, January 20, 1863.

Brigade composed of the 40th, 42d, 43d, 52d and, perhaps, the 41st Georgia regiments of infantry, and 1st regiment Georgia State Line, Stewart's division, Hood's corps, Army of Tennessee. Former command composed of the 1st, 3d and 4th Florida, 6th North Carolina and 47th Georgia regiments of infantry, Breckenridge's division. Commanding Preston's brigade, Army of Tennessee, May 25, 1863; commanding brigade in Breckenridge's division, Department of Mississippi and Eastern Louisiana, August, 1863. Died at Augusta, Ga., August 7, 1895.

STAFF.

Dearing, Wm. P., lieutenant A. D. C., September 1, 1864.

Dunham, Andrew, Jr., lieutenant ordance officer, March 9, 1863.

Hanson, A. J., lieutenant A. D. C., May 24, 1863.

Hull, Harvey H., captain A. I. G., 1861.

Hull, J. H., captain, September 19, 1863.

Triestra, Gregory, A. A. A. G., November 1, 1863.

Weakley, T. P., major A. C. S., September 1, 1862.

Webb, John, major A. Q. M., June 24, 1863.

Whitehead, J. P. C., Jr., captain A. A. G., May 24, 1863.

Evans, H., major C. S., December 18, 1863.

BRYAN MOREL THOMAS.

Cadet U. S. Military Academy, July 1, 1858; brevet 2d

lieutenant 8th infantry, July, 1858; 2d lieutenant 5th infantry, January 19, 1859; resigned April 6, 1861.

1st lieutenant corps of infantry, C. S. A., April 3, 1861; major corps of infantry, 1862; commanding 8th Alabama infantry —; commanding cavalry battalion of independent companies, 1864; commanding 12th Misisippi cavalry, 1864; brigadier-general, August 4, 1864.

Brigade composed of 1st Alabama Reserves, Col. Daniel E. Huger; 2d Alabama Reserves, Lieutenant-Colonel Junius A. Law; 21st Alabama regiment of infantry, Lieutenant-Colonel James M. Williams, District of the Gulf, General Dabney H. Maury commanding. Died at Dalton, Ga., July 16, 1905.

EDWARD L. THOMAS.

Colonel 35th Georgia regiment of infantry, October 15, 1861; brigadier-general, November 1, 1862.

Brigade composed of the 14th, 35th, 45th and 49th Georgia regiments of infantry, the 3d Louisiana battalion of infantry, and Captain Davidson's light battery of artillery, Pender's division, A. P. Hill's corps, Army of Northern Virginia. Died in Oklahoma, March 8, 1898.

STAFF.

Ginter, Lewis, major, October, 1862.

Norwood, William, lieutenant, October, 1862; captain A. A. G., April, 1863, November 4, 1864.

Tyler, John, lieutenant, October, 1862.

ROBERT TOOMBS.

Secretary of State, C. S. A., February 21, 1861; brigadier-general July 19, 1861; resigned March 4, 1863.

Brigade composed of the 2d, 15th, 17th and 20th Georgia regiments of infantry, and 1st regiment Georgia Regulars, Longstreet's corps, Army of Northern Virginia. Died at Washington, Ga., December 15, 1885.

STAFF.

Alexander, W. F., major A. Q. M., July 19, 1861; A. A. D. C., June, 1862.

Du Bose, D. M., captain A. A. G., June, 1862; captain A. D. C., October, 1862.

Erwin, John B., colonel Volunteer A. D. C.

Hill, A. A. F., captain 1st Georgia Regulars, A. A. D. C., Oct., 1862.

Lamar, G. De Rosset, captain A. D. C., October, 1862.

Troup, J. Robert, captain A. D. C., June, 1862.

Rains, T. A., senior surgeon December 31, 1862.

Hill, R. C., major A. A. G., August 9, 1861.
Lamar, W. T., captain ——, October, 1862.

DAVID EMANUEL TWIGGS.

Captain 8th infantry U. S. A., March, 1812; major 28th infantry, September, 1814; honorably discharged June 15, 1815. Reenlisted as captain 7th infantry December, 1815, with brevet of major from September 21, 1814; transferred to 1st infantry December 14, 1821; major May 14, 1825; lieutenant-colonel 4th infantry July 15, 1831; colonel 2d dragoons June 8, 1836; brigadier-general June 30, 1846; brevet major-general September 23, 1846, for gallant and meritorious conduct in the several conflicts at Monterey, Mexico. Received by resolution of the United States Congress March 20, 1847, the presentation of a sword "in testimony of the high sense entertained by Congress of his gallantry and good conduct in storming Monterey." Military governor of Vera Cruz, 1848; in command of the Department of Texas, February, 1861; joined the Confederacy.

Major-general P. A. C. S., May 22, 1861.

Commanding military District of Louisiana, April 17, 1861. Died July 15, 1862.

STAFF.

Beltzhoover D., major Louisiana artillery, A. A. A. G., June 1, 1861.

Devereaux, John G., 1st lieutenant artillery, A. A. A. G., August 6, 1861.

Devereaux, John D., lieutenant A. A. A. G., Aug. 28, 1861.

Hebert, P. O., colonel of artillery and chief of engineers, Feb. 19, 1861.

Haden, J. M., surgeon, Sept. 7, 1861.

Higgins, E., captain Louisiana artillery, A. D. C., June 1, 1861.

Major, James P., lieutenant A. D. C., June 1, 1861.

Manning, T. C., A. D. C., Aug., 1861.

Nichols, W. A., A. A. G., Feb 18, 1861.

Palfrey, E. A., captain A. C. S. and chief Commissary Department No. 1, July 24, 1861.

Smith, M. L., major of engineers, July 22, 1861.

Stickney, George W., chaplain, Sept. 21, 1861.

WILLIAM HENRY TALBOT WALKER.

Cadet U. S. Military Academy July 1, 1837; brevet 2d lieutenant 6th infantry July, 1837; 2d lieutenant July

31, 1837; 1st lieutenant February 1, 1838; brevet 1st lieutenant Dec. 25, 1837, for gallant and good conduct in war against the Florida Indians. Resigned Oct. 31, 1838 (?). 1st lieutenant 6th infantry November, 1840, to rank from February 1, 1838; captain November 7, 1845; commandant of cadets, U. S. Military Academy, 1854-'56; major 10th infantry March, 1855; brevet major August 20, 1847, for gallant and meritorious conduct in the battles of Contreras and Churubusco, Mexico, and lieutenant-colonel September 8, 1847, for gallant and meritorious conduct in the battle of Molino del Rey. Resigned December 20, 1860.

Major-general 1st division Georgia State volunteers April 25, 1861; brigadier-general May 25, 1861; resigned October 29, 1861. Intermediately, brigadier-general of Georgia State troops. Reappointed brigadier-general February 9, 1863; major-general May 23, 1863.

Assigned to command of 2d brigade at Pensacola, Fla., June 3, 1861; commanding 3d brigade 2d army corps, Army of the Mississippi; commanding division in D. H. Hill's corps, Army of Tennessee. Division composed of brigades of Liddell, Walthall, Ector and Wilson; afterwards of brigades of Mercer, Jackson, Gist and Stevens. In October 1863, division composed of brigades of Gregg, Gist and Wilson. Killed near Atlanta, Ga., February 22, 1864.

STAFF.

Anderson, R. H., captain A. D. C. and A. A. A. G., June, 1861.

Crump, S. H., captain A. I. G., Sept. 20, 1863.

Cumming, Joseph B., captain A. A. G., March 3, 1863.
NOTE.—We learn, unofficially, that Joseph B. Cumming, of Georgia, at the time of the battle of Chickamauga, September, 1863, was chief of staff, with rank of major, of the division of Major-General W. H. T. Walker. We are told, further, that he was assigned to the command of a battalion, with rank of lieutenant-colonel, early in 1865, but, the War ending, he never assumed specified command.

Dearing, Alfred L., major A. C. S., April 30, 1862.

Lamar, G. De Rosset, lieutenant A. D. C., May 3, 1863.

Magruder, Lawson W., 2d lieutenant ordnance officer, May 2, 1863.

Talbot, M. H., captain volunteer A. D. C., Sept. 20, 1863.

Tilton, Nathaniel O., major A. Q. M., May 2, 1863.

Troup, S. Robert, captain A. A. G., May 3, 1863.

Heard, T. R., major Q. M., September 17, 1863.

Jackson, Henry, 2d lieutenant A. D. C., January, 1863.

HENRY C. WAYNE.

Cadet U. S. Military Academy, July 1, 1838; promoted 1st lieutenant 1st artillery May 16, 1842; on quartermaster duty during war with Mexico, 1846-'47; brevetted major for gallantry at Battles of Churubusco and Contreras; connected with quartermaster dept. from 1848 to 1860; resigned from U. S. Army in 1860.

Adjutant and inspector-general of the State of Georgia, with rank of colonel, November 12, 1860. Adjutant and inspector-general of the State of Georgia, with rank of major-general, November 30, 1861. Brigadier-general P. A. C. S., December 16, 1861; declined the appointment. Died, March 15, 1883.

NOTE.—Among General Wayne's notable colleagues on Governor Brown's military staff during the War was Hon. Ira R. Foster, Georgia's efficient Quartermaster-General.

JOSEPH WHEELER.

Cadet U. S. Military Academy, July 1, 1859; brevet 2d lieutenant 1st dragoons, July 1, 1859; transferred to mounted rifles June 26, 1860; 2d lieutenant September 1, 1860. Resigned April 22, 1861.

1st lieutenant corps of artillery, C. S. A., April 3, 1861; colonel 19th regiment Alabama volunteers September 4, 1861; brigadier-general October 30, 1862; major-general January 20, 1863.

It has been unofficially claimed that General Joseph Wheeler was, before the close of the War, promoted to the grade of lieutenant-general, P. A. C. S. The War Department, Washington, D. C., has this to say on the subject of his rank: "The parole roll of General Joseph Wheeler, C. S. Army, has not been found on file, but to a letter to General Halleck, dated from the steamer W. P. Clide, near Fort Monroe, Va., May 20, 1865, in which he asked to be released on parole, he signs himself 'J. Wheeler, Major-General, C. S. Army.'"

Brigade composed of the 17th, 18th and 19th Alabama regiments, and 2d Texas regiment, April, 1862. Assigned to cavalry July 18, 1862. Brigade composed of 1st and 2d Mississippi regiments, 1st and 3d Alabama regiments, 2d Arkansas regiment and 8th Confederate regiment from July 20 to August 16, 1862. Brigade composed of 1st and 3d Alabama regiments until September 16, when it was reinforced by 1st Kentucky, 1st Confederate, and 3d Georgia regiments. Oct. 1, 1862, in command of cavalry in Kentucky. Oct. 13, chief of cavalry of department;

command consisting of brigades of Colonels John H. Morgan, John A. Wharton, and the old Wheeler brigade, commanded by Colonel W. W. Allen. Nov. 20, chief of cavalry, Army of Tennessee; command composed of old brigade commanded by Colonel Jas. Hagan, and brigade of brigadier-general John A. Wharton; after December 20, 1863, of brigade of Brigadier-general John Pegram. January 20 in command of cavalry, Army of Tennessee, composed of bridgades of Brigadier-generals N. B. Forrest, John A. Wharton, Wm. T. Martin and John H. Morgan; Mch. 15, 1863, commanding army corps of cavalry composed of divisions of Brigadier-generals Jno. H. Morgan, W. T. Martin and John A. Wharton, each division composed of two brigades. Jnne 20, 1863, Morgan's division detached. Sept. 28, 1863, in command of cavalry, Army of Tennessee, composed of the divisions of Brigadier-generals Wm. T. Martin, John A. Wharton and H. B. Davidson. November 20, 1863, corps composed of divisions of Major-generals John A. Wharton, Wm. T. Martin, John H. Kelly, and Brigadier-general Frank C. Armstrong; November 27 Martin's and Armstrong's divisions detached. November 30, 1863, command composed of General Kelly's division, comprising Allen's and Grigsby's brigades, and Davidson's division, composed of Humes' and Ashby's brigades. May 10, 1864, command composed of Major-general Martin's division, comprising Brigadier-generals Iverson's and John T. Morgan's brigades; Brigadier-general Humes' division, comprising brigades of Harrison and Colonel McKensie; Brigadier-general Kelly's division, comprising brigades of Ashby and Allen, afterwards Anderson's; also the brigade of Brigadier-general John S. Williams, formerly Grigsby's brigade; Brigadier-general Wm .H. Jackson's division, comprising brigades of Ferguson, Armstrong and Ross, directed to report directly to Gen'l Jos. E. Johnston, but was often under Gen'l Wheeler's command. August 10, 1864, command consisted of divisions of Gen'l W. W. Allen (formerly Martin's), W. Y. C. Humes and J. H. Kelly, and brigade of Brigadier-general John S. Williams; August 22, 1864, Kelly's division, Williams' brigade and Dibrell's brigade of Humes' division were detached, remaining absent in West Virginia until November 30. November 30, command composed of divisions of Brigadier-general W. W. Allen, comprising brigades of Colonel C. C. Crews and James Hagan; Brigadier-general W. Y. C. Humes' division, comprising brigades of General Thos.

Harrison and Colonel Ashby; Brigadier-general Alfred Iverson's division, composed of brigades of Brigadier-general S. W. Ferguson and Joseph H. Lewis.

Died at Brooklyn Heights, N. Y., January 25, 1906.

STAFF.

Bellinger, John, 2d lieutenant A. D. C., July 1, 1864.

Brewer, R., captain A. D. C., December, 1863. Killed June, 1864.

Burford, E. S., 1st lieutenant A. A. G., Oct. 30, 1862; major, A. A. G., January 20, 1863.

Clawston, J. G., lieutenant A. D. C., July, 1863.

Chaffie, O. P., major Q. M., May 20, 1863.

Chapman, Henry, 2d lieutenant I. G., Dec. 10, 1864.

Cochran, J. W., lieutenant I. G. March 1, 1864; provisional lieutenant colonel.

Dunlap, W. W., lieutenant-colonel A. D. C., June 27, 1863.

Elliott, Samuel N., major A. D. C. March 1, 1865.

Elmore, Vincent M., captain inspector-general Dec. 26, 1862; provisional major.

Garnett, O. V., captain assistant surgeon March 7, 1862.

Gibbons, J. L., captain A. Q. M. March 4, 1865.

Grenfel, G. St. Leger, lieutenant-colonel volunteer A. D. C. Dec. 30, 1862; lieutenant-colonel, inspector-general March 1, 1863.

Grigsby, J. Warren, colonel chief of staff Jan.-March, 1863, Jan. 14, 1865.

Harris, Wm. Hooper, captain A. Q. M. Dec. 10, 1862; 2d lieutenant inspector-general Oct. 30, 1862, and A. D. C. Jan. 20, 1863.

Hill, William E., lieutenant inspector-general 1862.

Hodgson, Telfair, captain volunteer A. D. C., Dec. 21, 1862.

Hudson, Marcellus G., lieutenant A. D. C. July 1, 1863; promoted major adjutant-general Nov., 1864.

Humes, W. Y. C., major chief artillery March 15, 1863; promoted brigadier-general Nov. 16, 1863.

Jenkins, D. C., major inspector-general July 10, 1864.

Jones, Thomas M., lieutenant ordn. department, July, 1863.

Kerr, S. P., captain ordnance officer, July 1, 1863.

Kidd, Joseph, captain A. Q. M. July 20, 1862.

King, Hugh M., colonel A. D. C. Jan. 3, 1863.

Labouisse, John W., captain A. A. & I. G., July 3, 1864.

101

Lacy, Richard F., 2d lieutenant A. D. C. and engineer May 3, 1863.

Ledyard, Edward S., lieutenant volunteer A. D. C., Dec. 25, 1863.

Lewis, Earnest S., major surgeon Oct. 7, 1864.

Lowery, David, lieutenant A. D. C. Dec. 12, 1862; killed Oct. 27, 1864.

Lynch, Frank, major surgeon Nov., 1862.

Martin, Andrew B., 2d lieutenant A. A. G. Dec. 15, 1864.

McGuirk, John, lieutenant-colonel volunteer A. D. C. Oct., 1862; A. A. G. Sept. 26, 1862.

McIntire, Hamilton, lieutenant A. D. C. Dec. 18, 1862.

Norris, ——, 2d lieutenant A. A. G. Feb. 2, 1865.

Norton, Sam. E., captain Q. M. Sept. 1, 1862; promoted major.

Parker, W. A., lieutenant ordnance officer Feb. 1, 1865.

Patton, ——, 2d lieutenant A. D. C. Aug. 25, 1863. Killed Sept. 12, 1863.

Patterson, James, 2d lieutenant A. D. C. Killed June 16, 1863.

Pointer, E., 2d lieutenant A. D. C. Feb. 28, 1864. Killed March 10, 1864.

Pointer, Marcellus, lieutenant A. D. C. July 18, 1862; wounded and transferred to hospital Oct., 1863; promoted lieutenant-colonel 12th Alabama Dec., 1864.

Powell, Thos. E., captain inspector-general Jan. 20, 1863.

Prentice, Clarence J., major volunteer A. D. C., Dec. 1, 1862.

Raffin, Wm., captain A. C. S. July 20, 1862.

Rawle, Ed., captain inspector-general June 1, 1863.

Reed, Duff G., captain A. A. G. Aug. 10, 1862.

Reese, Warren S., captain I. G. Nov. 30, 1862. Killed.

Robertson, F. H., lieutenant-colonel chief artillery Jan. 1, 1864; promoted brigadier-general July 26, 1864; wounded and permanently disabled Nov. 28, 1864.

Rogers, Charles G., lieutenant colonel I. G. June 1, 1863.

Rudd, I., captain volunteer A. D. C. Nov. 1, 1862. Killed Nov. 27, 1862.

Ryan, R. B., lieutenant engineer officer, Nov. 20, 1864.

Saunders, D. D., captain assistant surgeon Sept. 1, 1861.

Shannon, A. N., lieutenant-colonel chief of scouts March 2, 1865.

Sparks, Wm. H., captain A. D. C. May 20, 1864. Killed July 22, 1864.

Stafford, J. C., lieutenant A. D. C. June 21, 1864.

Stanford, Frank A., major surgeon Dec. 21, 1862.

Staples, Thomas J., lieutenant A. D. C. July 3, 1864. Killed July 22, 1864.

Steele, S. W., captain engineers, Nov. 1, 1862.

Stewart, J. M., 2d lieutenant engineer Dec. 16, 1864.

Taylor, George L., lieutenant A. D. C. Nov. 12, 1862. Killed Dec. 27, 1862.

Thomas, Breck C. (G.?), major chief com'y Jan. 30, 1863.

Tracy, E. D., lieutenant-colonel A. A. G. July 20, 1862. Promoted brigadier-general.

Turner, Geo., captain inspector general May 1, 1863.

Wailes, Wm. E., major adjutant-general Sept., 1864. Lieutenant A. D. C. Aug. 30, 1862; wounded and transferred to hospital Jan. 5, 1863.

Walker, Clifton, lieutenant A. D. C. July 20, 1862.

Warren, Herbert C., 2d lieutenant ordnance department Aug. 20, 1864.

Watkins, J. C., captain A. D. C. Feb. 20, 1864. Killed July 22, 1864.

CLAUDIUS C. WILSON.

Colonel 25th Georgia regiment of infantry September 2, 1861; brigadier-general November 16, 1863.

Brigade composed of the 13th, 25th, 29th and 30th Georgia regiments of infantry, the 1st battalion Georgia Sharpshooters and the 4th Louisiana battalion of infantry, Army of Tennessee. Died November 24, 1863.

STAFF.

Bacon, W. D., captain and A. Q. M.

Lester, Rufus E., captain and A. A. G.

WILLIAM T. WOFFORD.

Colonel 18th Georgia regiment of infantry 1862; brigadier-general January 17, 1863.

Brigade composed of the 16th, 18th and 24th Georgia regiments of infantry, Cobb's Georgia Legion, Phillips' Georgia Legion, and 3d battalion Georgia Sharpshooters, McLaws' division, Longstreet's corps, Army of Northern Virginia.

Died May 22, 1884.

STAFF.

Woolley, A. F., captain A. A. G. Nov. 4, 1864.

Hackett, J. T., captain A. A. G., Dec. 9, 1863.

Patton, A. H., captain A. A. G., February 17, 1863.

Wofford, W. L., lieutenant A. D. C., May 25, 1863.
Lumkin, F., captain A. Q. M., April 29, 1864.

AMBROSE RANSOM WRIGHT.

Colonel 3d Georgia regiment of infantry May 8, 1861; colonel 38th Georgia Infantry, October 15, 1861; resigned April 23, 1962; Brigadier-General, June 3, 1862; general, November 26, 1864.

Brigade composed of the 3d, 22d, 46th and 48th Georgia regiments of infantry, and 2d Georgia battalion, Anderson's division, A. P. Hill's corps, Army of Northern Virginia.

Division composed of the brigades of Mercer and John K. Jackson.

Died December 21, 1872.

STAFF.

Bell, R. H., captain A. D. C. at the battle of Chancellorsville, May 3, 1863.

Dickinson, A. G., captain A. A. G. June, 1862.

Girardey, V. J. B., captain A. A. G. June-July, 1862; battle of Chancellorsville, May 3, 1863.

Hazlehurst, Wm., lieutenant A. D. C. at battle of Chancellorsville, May 3, 1863.

Perry, W. H., captain A. A. G. Nov. 4, 1864.

Snead, Claiborne, captain A. A. G. May 17, 1863.

Whitehead, Chas. L., captain volunteer A. D. C., June-July, 1862.

Beall, Julius, C. A., captain A. D. C., May 3, 1863.

NOTE.—**Colonel Francis Stebbins Bartow,** of 8th Georgia Infantry, who fell at First Battle of Manassas, Va., July 21, 1861, and **Colonel Edward S. Willis,** of 12th Georgia Infantry, who fell in affair at Bethesda Church, Va., May 30, 1864, were both gallant officers, and, had they lived, would, doubtless, have been promoted to the grade of brigadier-general, P. A. C. S.

GILBERT J. WRIGHT.

Appointed from Georgia. A colonel (of Cavalry Battalion, Cobb's Georgia Legion, and of the 9th Georgia cavalry,) in command of General P. M. B. Young's old brigade. He was, on promotion of General Young to grade of major-general, P. A. C. S., in Dec., 1864, assigned to this brigade. His brigade was composed of the Cobb and Phillips Georgia Legions, the Jeff Davis Mississippi Legion, the 10th Georgia cavalry regiment, and Millen's 20th battalion of Georgia Partisan Rangers—all cavalry commands—Army of Northern Virginia. Died June 3, 1905.

If Colonel Gilbert J. Wright had a staff, it was that of the former brigadier-general commanding, General P. M. B. Young. There is no record of any appointed by himself.

PIERCE MANNING BUTLER YOUNG.

Second lieutenant corps of artillery C. S. A., April, 1861; first lieutenant corps of artillery, C. S. A., June, 1861; aide-de-camp to General W. H. T. Walker; first lieutenant and adjutant Cobb's Legion, July 24, 1861; major Cobb's Legion, Sept. 5, 1861; lieutenant-colonel Cobb's Legion, Nov. 15, 1862; colonel Cobb's Legion, Dec., 1862; brigadier-general Sept. 28, 1863; major-general Dec. 30, 1864.

Brigade composed of Cobb's Legion, the Jeff Davis Legion, Phillips' Legion and 7th Georgia cavalry (all cavalry), Hampton's division, Army of Northern Virginia. In November, 1864, the 10th regiment Georgia cavalry was substituted for the 7th Georgia cavalry, and Millen's battalion of Georgia cavalry was added. Division composed of the brigades of Lewis, Ferguson and Harrison.

Died in New York City July 6, 1896.

STAFF.

Church, William L., captain A. A. G. 1863; promoted major May, 1864, March, 1865.

Edelin, Thos. Boyd, captain A. I. G., 1863; promoted major; afterwards colonel 6th North Carolina cavalry.

Glenn, John W., captain ordnance officer, 1864.

Jones, John M., lieutenant A. D. C. 1863; promoted to captain 1864.

Lumpkin, Miller G., major com'y 1863.

Palmer, ——, Doctor division, captain, chaplain.

Thomas, J. P., lieutenant A. D. C., 1864.

Williams, Thomas H., captain A. Q. M.; promoted major.

OFFICERS OF THE CONFEDERATE STATES NAVY APPOINTED FROM GEORGIA, 1861-1865.

(NOTE.—In many instances the records do not disclose the State from which the officer was appointed; hence, there will be omissions.)

ANDERSON, EDWIN M.

Born in Georgia. Midshipman, November 18, 1861. Midshipman Provisional Navy, June 2, 1864.

Abroad 1862-4; C. S. S. Alabama, 1864.

ANDREWS, WILLIAM.

Born in Georgia. Acting midshipman July 20, 1861. Killed at Gibraltar on C. S. S. Sumter, October 15, 1862, by Acting Master's Mate J. T. Hester, C. S. Navy.

ARMSTRONG, AENEAS.

Born in Georgia. Resigned as lieutenant U. S. Navy, November 21, 1860. First lieutenant, April 24, 1862. Dismissed January 9, 1864. First lieutenant, Provisional Navy (nominated), to rank from July 26, 1864.

Served on C. S. S. Sampson, 1863. C. S. S. Fredericksburg, 1865. Drowned in the sinking of steam packet boat Hornet by collision with steamer Allison.

ARMSTRONG, RICHARD FIELDER.

Born in Georgia. Resigned as acting midshipman, U. S. Navy, January 30, 1861. Midshipman, April 17, 1861. Acting master, September 24, 1861. Lieutenant for the war, February 8, 1862. Second lieutenant, October 23, 1862, to rank from October 2, 1862. First lieutenant Provisional Navy, June 2, 1864, to rank from January 6, 1864.

Served on C. S. S. Sumter, 1861-2; C. S. S. Alabama, 1864; assisted in the defense of Battery Buchanan in the attack by the Union forces upon Fort Fisher, December 23-25, 1864; gallant conduct commended.

BAILEY, JOHN H.

Born in Georgia. Third assistant engineer June 15,

1861. Second assistant engineer Provisional Navy, June 2, 1864.

Naval station, Savannah, Ga., 1863. C. S. S. Richmond, 1864.

BERRIEN, THOMAS M.

Born in Georgia. Resigned as acting midshipman (U. S. N.), January 26, 1861. Acting midshipman, July 8, 1861. Midshipman Provisional Navy June 2, 1864. Passed midshipman Provisional Navy (date not given).

Served on C. S. S. Savannah, 1863. Schoolship Patrick Henry, 1864. C. S. S. Chickamauga, 1864. Ordered to C. S. S. Macon, August 19, 1864.

BORCHERT, GEORGE A.

Born in Georgia. Formerly midshipman, U. S. Navy. Midshipman, July 25, 1861. Master, July 25, 1861. Second lieutenant, February 8, 1862. First lieutenant, January 7, 1864, to rank from October 2, 1862. First lieutenant Provisional Navy, June 2, 1864, to rank from January 6, 1864.

Served on C. S. S. Baltic, 1862-3. C. S. S. Rappahannock, 1863-4. Abroad, 1864. Ordered to C. S. S. Stonewall, January 10, 1865. Killed in Central America (date not given).

BULLOCH, JAMES D.

Born in Georgia. Resigned as lieutenant, U. S. Navy, October 5, 1854. Commander for the war, October 23, 1862, to rank from January 17, 1862. Commander Provisional Navy (nominated), to rank from May 13, 1864.

Ordered to command steamer Fingal, November 10, 1861. Special service abroad, as financial agent of the Navy Department, 1862-4.

BULLOCH, JAMES D., JR.

Born in Georgia. Midshipman, August 29, 1861. Midshipman Provisional Navy, June 2, 1864.

Served on C. S. S. Alabama, 1862-3. Abroad, 1863-4.

CARTER, BARRON.

Born in Georgia. Resigned as acting midshipman, U. S. Navy, January 25, 1861. Acting midshipman, July 8, 1861. Midshipman Provisional Navy, June 2, 1864.

Served on C. S. S. Georgia, 1862-3. C. S. S. Isondiga; detached and ordered to C. S. S. Savannah, August 19, 1863. C. S. S. Patrick Henry, 1863-4.

CHARLTON, THOMAS J.

Born in Georgia. Resigned as assistant surgeon, U. S. Navy, December 18, 1860. Assistant surgeon, April 2, 1862. Passed assistant surgeon, September 13, 1862. Passed assistant surgeon Provisional Navy, June 2, 1864.

Served on C. S. S. Georgia, 1862. Special service abroad, 1863-4. C. S. S. Florida, 1864; prisoner on U. S. S. Wachusett, October 7, 1864.

CHASE, WILLIAM H.

Born in Georgia. Assistant paymaster, February 26, 1863. Assistant paymaster Provisional Navy, June 2, 1864.

Special service under Commander Frederick Chatard, C. S. Navy, 1864.

CLAYTON, WILLIAM FORCE.

Born in Georgia. Acting midshipman, October 5, 1861. Midshipman Provisional Navy, June 2, 1864. Passed midshipman Provisional Navy.

Served on C. S. S. Richmond, 1862-3. C. S. S. Patrick Henry, 1864. Savannah Squadron; C. S. S. Georgia; detached September 1, 1864, and ordered to C. S. S. Sampson; ordered to C. S. S. Macon, March 22, 1865.

COHEN, M. J.

Born in Georgia. Third assistant engineer July 29, 1863. Third assistant engineer Provisional Navy, June 2, 1864.

Served on C. S. S. Palmetto State, 1863-4. Charleston Squadron, 1864.

DANIEL, GEORGE C.

Born in ———. Assistant surgeon Provisional Navy, (nominated), September 6, 1864.

Semmes Naval Brigade, 1865.

DIGGERS, GEORGE.

Born in Georgia. Third assistant engineer November 28, 1863.

Special service, 1863-4.

FLOURNOY, ROBERT.

Born in Georgia. Resigned as acting midshipman, U. S. Navy, January 12, 1861. Acting midshipman, July 8, 1861. Resigned, July 9, 1864.

Served on C. S. S. Georgia, 1862-3.

FORD, THEODOSIUS BARTOW.

Born in Georgia. Assistant surgeon, May 15, 1861. Assistant surgeon, October 23, 1862, to rank from October 2, 1862. Assistant surgeon Provisional Navy, June 2, 1864.

Served on C. S. S. Gaines, 1862-3. Ordered from C. S. S. Resolute to C. S. S. Isondiga, December 11, 1863, on temporary duty. C. S. S. Savannah, 1863-4. C. S. S. Isondiga, May 13, 1864. C. S. S. Sampson, February 28, 1865.

FOSTER, J. L.

Born in Georgia. Second assistant engineer, December 29, 1862. Second assistant engineer, May 21, 1863. Second assistant engineer Provisional Navy, June 2, 1864.

Served on C. S. S. Isondiga, 1863-4.

GRAVES, CHARLES J.

Born in Georgia. Formerly lieutenant, U. S. Navy. First lieutenant, December 27, 1861. First lieutenant, October 23, 1863 (2?), to rank from October 2, 1862. First lieutenant, Provisional Navy, June 2, 1864, to rank from January 6, 1864.

Served on C. S. S. Morgan, 1862-3. Special service abroad, 1863-4. C. S. S. Virginia (No. 2); flag lieutenant to Flag Officer John K. Mitchell, 1865.

GRAVES, HENRY L.

Born in Georgia. Second lieutenant Marine Corps, October 24, 1862. First lieutenant Marine Corps (nominated), December, 1863.

Served on C. S. S. Savannah; order dated July 20, 1863. Ordered February 1, 1864, to report to Flag Officer Tattnall, commanding Savannah station.

GREENHOW, J. W. B.

Born in Georgia. Formerly passed assistant surgeon, U. S. Navy. Surgeon, August 2, 1861. Surgeon, October 23, 1862, to rank from March 26, 1861. Surgeon Provisional Navy, June 2, 1864.

Prisoner; paroled off Roanoke Island, N. C., February 12, 1862. Naval station, Wilmington, N. C., 1863-4. Fleet surgeon, Wilmington, N. C., 1864.

HALL, WILBURN B.

Born in South Carolina. Resigned as midshipman, U. S. Navy, March 7, 1861. Acting midshipman, April 16,

1861. Master, July 24, 1861. Acting lieutenant, September 19, 1861. Lieutenant for the war, February 8, 1862. First lieutenant, February 8, 1862. First lieutenant October 23, 1863 (2?), to rank from October 2, 1862. First lieutenant Provisional Navy, June 2, 1864, to rank from January 6, 1864.

Served on C. S. Steamers Huntress and Savannah, 1861; Tuscaloosa, 1862-3; C. S. S. Patrick Henry, 1863-4; C. S. steamers Raleigh, Roanoke, Drewry and Virginia (No. 2), James River Squadron, 1864.

HERTY, JAMES W.

Born in Georgia. Formerly assistant surgeon, U. S. Navy. Assistant surgeon (nominated), February 10, 1862. Passed assistant surgeon, October 25, 1862. Passed assistant surgeon Provisional Navy, June 2, 1864.

Prisoner at Hampton Roads, 1861; paroled, 1862. C. S. S. Richmond, 1862-3. C. S. S. Rappahannock, 1863-4. C. S. S. Stonewall, 1865.

HOLCOMB, ISAAC C.

Born in Georgia. Resigned as acting midshipman, U. S. Navy, January 19, 1861. Acting midshipman, May 16, 1861. Passed midshipman, October 3, 1862. Master in line of promotion, January 7, 1864. Second lieutenant Provisional Navy, June 2, 1864.

Served on C. S. S. Savannah, 1862-3. Special service abroad, 1863-4.

JOHNSON, WILBUR F.

Born in ———. Second lieutenant Marine Corps, June 29, 1861. First lieutenant Marine Corps (date not given). Resigned July 4, 1862.

JOHNSTON, E. J.

(Also found as Edward J. Johnson.)
Born in Georgia. First assistant engineer, April 29, 1862. Died, October 14, 1863.

Served on C. S. S., Atlanta, Savannah Squadron, 1862-3.

JONES, C. LUCIAN.

Born in District of Columbia. Original entry into C. S. Navy, November 29, 1862. Assistant paymaster, January 7, 1864, to rank from November 29, 1862. Assistant paymaster Provisional Navy, June 2, 1864.

Secretary to flag officer commanding Savannah Squadron, 1863. C. S. S. North Carolina, 1863-4. C. S. S. Tallahassee, 1864.

KELL, JOHN McINTOSH.

Born in Georgia. Resigned as lieutenant, U. S. Navy, January 23, 1861. First lieutenant, March 26, 1861. First lieutenant, October 23, 1862, to rank from October 2, 1862. Commander Provisional Navy (nominated), June, 1864, to rank from October 4, 1863.

Served on C. S. S. Sumter, 1861-2. C. S. S. Alabama, 1863-4. Commanding C. S. S. Richmond, 1865.

LOW, JOHN.

Born in Georgia. Master not in line of promotion, November 5, 1861. Lieutenant for the war, January 7, 1864, to rank from August 25, 1863. First lieutenant Provisional Navy, June 2, 1864, to rank from January 6, 1864.

Ordered by Commander J. D. Bulloch, March 21, 1862, to take passage in the C. S. S. Florida to superintend her transfer to the C. S. Government. C. S. S. Alabama, 1862-3. C. S. S. Tuscaloosa (also called Conrad, tender to C. S. S. Alabama), June 21, 1863-January 9, 1864.

LUDDINGTON, W. A.

Born in Georgia. Third assistant engineer July 4, 1863. Third assistant engineer Provisional Navy, June 2, 1864.

Served on C. S. S. Resolute, 1863-4. C. S. S. Torch, 1864.

McCARTHY, L. A.

Born in Georgia. Original entry into C. S. Navy, December 29, 1862. Second assistant engineer, May 21, 1863.

Served on C. S. S. Savannah, Savannah Squadron, 1863-4.

McDONALD, DONALD.

Born in Georgia. Third assistant engineer, July 20, 1863. Third assistant engineer Provisional Navy, June 2, 1864.

Served on C. S. S. Charleston, 1863-4. Ordered to C. S. S. Isondiga, September 23, 1864.

McGRATH, J. W.

Born in Georgia. Third assistant engineer, August 5, 1863. Resigned January 12, 1864. Third assistant engineer Provisional Navy, June 2, 1864.

Served on C. S. S. Savannah, December 7, 1863-4.

MERIWETHER, JAMES A.

Born in Georgia. Resigned as acting midshipman, U. S. Navy, January 22, 1861. Acting midshipman, May 16, 1861. Passed midshipman, October 3, 1862. Resigned February 11, 1863.

Served on C. S. S. Gaines, 1862-3.

MAFFITT, EUGENE A.

Born in Georgia. Acting midshipman, November 16, 1861. Midshipman, Provisional Navy, June 2, 1864.

Served on C. S. S. Alabama, 1862-4.

MORRIS, CHARLES MANIGAULT.

Born in South Carolina. Resigned as lieutenant, U. S. Navy, January 29, 1861. First lieutenant, March 26, 1861. First lieutenant, October 23, 1862, to rank from October 2, 1862. First lieutenant Provisional Navy, June 2, 1864, to rank from January 6, 1864.

Naval rendevous, Savannah, Ga., 1862-3. Commanding C. S. S. Florida from January, 1864, till captured in Bahia Harbor, Brazil, October 7, 1864.

MOSES, RAPHAEL J.

Born in Florida. Resigned as acting midshipman, U. S. Navy, January 23, 1861. Acting midshipman, July 8, 1861. Midshipman Provisional Navy, June 2, 1864. Master in line of promotion (nominated), November, 1864.

Savannah Squadron, 1862-3. Abroad, 1864. Assigned to Battery Semmes, James River, October, 1864.

MYERS, HENRY.

Born in Georgia. Resigned as paymaster, U. S. Navy, February 1, 1861. Paymaster, March 26, 1861. Paymaster, October 23, 1862, to rank from March 26, 1861.

Served on C. S. S. Sumter, 1861-2. Charleston Squadron, 1862-4.

MYERS, JULIAN.

Born in Georgia. Formerly lieutenant, U. S. Navy. First lieutenant, February 6, 1862. First lieutenant, October 23, 1862, to rank from October 2, 1862. First lieutenant Provisional Navy, June 2, 1864, to rank from January 6, 1864.

Served on C. S. S. Huntsville, 1862-3. Commanding Tuscaloosa, Mobile Squadron, 1864. Commanding C. S.

S. Huntsville, November, 1864. Surrendered May 4, 1865; paroled May 10, 1865.

NEUFVILLE, EDWARD F.

Born in Georgia. Second lieutenant, Marine Corps, March 6, 1863.

Savannah Squadron, 1863-4. Detached from C. S. S. Savannah, August 1, 1864.

NORRIS, JAMES R.

Born in Georgia. Acting midshipman, October 6, 1861. Midshipman Provisional Navy, June 2, 1864.

Served on C. S. S. Morgan, 1862-3. C. S. S. Patrick Henry, 1863-4.

READ, JACOB.

Born in ———. Resigned as first lieutenant, U. S. Marine Corps, February 28, 1861. Captain, Marine Corps (date not given). Dismissed, February 1, 1863.

SEYMOUR, DEWITT C.

Born in Georgia. Assistant paymaster, October 20, 1862. Assistant paymaster Provisional Navy, June 2, 1864.

Served on C. S. S. Georgia, 1862-4.

SINCLAIR, ARTHUR, JR.

Born in Georgia. Master not in line of promotion, April 1, 1862. Lieutenant for the war, January 7, 1864, to rank from August 25, 1863. First lieutenant Provisional Navy, June 2, 1864, to rank from January 6, 1864.

Served on C. S. R. S. United States, Gosport Navy Yard, 1861, as master's mate. C. S. S. Alabama, 1862-4.

SMITH, IRA E.

Born in ———. Assistant surgeon Provisional Navy (nominated), November, 1864.

STILES, RANDOLPH R.

Born in ———. Entered Confederate service as a private in the Richmond Howitzers July 20, 1861. Wounded at the battle of Cold Harbor, June, 1863. Second lieutenant Provisional Navy (date not given).

Served on C. S. S. Richmond, 1865.

TIFT, NELSON.

Born in —— assistant paymaster (nominated), to rank from Oct. 1, 1864.

"Mr. Nelson Tift is nominated for the appointment of assistant paymaster to take charge of and superintend the naval flour mills and bakery at Albany, Ga., and to act as disbursing officer for the same." (President's Message, Nov. 9, 1864.)

TATTNALL, JOHN R. F.

Born in Connecticut. Formerly first lieutenant, U. S. Marine Corps. Captain Marine Corps, January 22, 1862. Savannah, Ga., 1863-4.

TATTNALL, JOSIAH.

Born in Georgia. Resigned as captain, U. S. Navy, February 21, 1861. Captain, March 26, 1861. ·Captain, October 23, 1862, to rank from March 26, 1861.

In charge of naval defenses of South Carolina and Georgia, 1862. Commanding C. S. S. Virginia (Merrimack), 1862. Commandant, Savannah, 1862-3.

TIPTON, JOSEPH S.

Born in Georgia. Assistant surgeon, May 1, 1863. Assistant surgeon Provisional Navy, June 2, 1864.

Naval station, Wilmington, N. C., 1863-4. Captured, May 5, 1864, in C. S. S. Bombshell, in Albemarle Sound, N. C. Ordered to C. S. S. Isondiga, September 21, 1864; detached September 26, 1864, and ordered to duty on board C. S. steamers Resolute and Firefly.

WAYNE, WILLIAM A.

Born in Georgia. Resigned as lieutenant, U. S. Navy, May 1, 1861. First lieutenant, June 20, 1861. Died August 4, 1863.

Gosport Navy Yard, 1861-2.

WILKES, G. G.

Born in Georgia. Midshipman, October 14, 1862. Midshipman Provisional Navy, June 2, 1864.

Savannah station, 1862-3.

WILKINS, G. A.

Born in Georgia. Midshipman, October 14, 1862. Midshipman Provisional Navy, June 2, 1864.

Charleston Squadron, 1863-'64.

YONGE, BRAGG.

Born in Georgia. Third assistant engineer, April 27, 1863.

Served on C. S. S. Savannah, 1863-4.

MEMBERS OF THE CONFEDERATE STATES CONGRESS FROM GEORGIA.

Provisional Congress.

First session assembled at Montgomery, Ala., February 4, 1861. Adjourned March 16, 1861, to meet second Monday in May.

Second session (called) met at Montgomery, Ala., April 29, 1861. Adjourned May 21, 1861.

Third session met at Richmond, Va., July 20, 1861. Adjourned August 31, 1861.

Fourth session (called) met at Richmond, Va., September 3, 1861. Adjourned same day.

Fifth session met at Richmond, Va., November 18, 1861. Adjourned February 17, 1862.

MEMBERS FROM GEORGIA.

Francis S. Bartow. Killed at Manassas, Va., July 21, 1861.
Nathan Bass. Admitted January 14, 1862.
Howell Cobb.
Thomas R. R. Cobb.
Martin J. Crawford.
Thomas M. Foreman. Admitted August 7, 1861.
Benjamin H. Hill.
Augustus H. Kenan.
Eugenius A. Nisbet.
Alexander H. Stephens.
Robert Toombs.
Augustus R. Wright.

It is interesting to remember that Hon. Howell Cobb, of Georgia, afterward major-general, P. A. C. S., was the president of this memorable Confederate Provisional Congress. He was, as we understand, an admirable presiding officer, and worthily represented his native State. He was one of the notable members of his delegation.

First Congress.

First session met at Richmond, Va., February 18, 1862. Adjourned April 21, 1862.

Second session met at Richmond, Va., August 18, 1862. Adjourned October 13, 1862.

Third session met at Richmond, Va., January 12, 1863. Adjourned May 1, 1863.

Fourth session met at Richmond, Va., December 7, 1863. Adjourned February 17, 1864.

SENATORS FROM GEORGIA.

Benjamin H. Hill.

Hershel V. Johnson. Admitted January 19, 1863.

John W. Lewis. Admitted April 7, 1862. Appointed by the Governor.

REPRESENTATIVES FROM GEORGIA.

William W. Clark.

Lucius J. Gartrell.

Julian Hartridge. Admitted March 14, 1862.

Hines, Holt. Resigned previous to January 12, 1864.

Porter Ingram. Admitted January 12, 1864. Succeeded Hines Holt.

Augustus H. Kenan.

David W. Lewis.

Charles J. Munnerlyn. Admitted February 22, 1862.

Hardy Strickland.

Robert P. Trippe.

Augustus R. Wright.

Second Congress.

First session met at Richmond, Va., May 2, 1864. Adjourned June 14, 1864.

Second session met at Richmond, Va., November 7, 1864. Adjourned March 18, 1865.

SENATORS FROM GEORGIA.

Benjamin H. Hill.

Herschel V. Johnson. Admitted May 24, 1864.

REPRESENTATIVES FROM GEORGIA.

Warren Akin.

Clifford Anderson.

Hiram P. Bell.

Mark H. Blandford.

Joseph H. Echols.

Julian Hartridge.

George N. Lester.

John T. Shewmake.

James M. Smith.

William E. Smith.

CONFEDERATE CABINET OFFICERS, APPOINTED FROM GEORGIA.

HON. ROBERT TOOMBS, of Georgia, served as the first Secretary of State of Confederate Government from February 21 to July 21, 1861. HON. WM. M. BROWNE, of Georgia, afterwards Colonel A. D. C., on military staff of President Davis, and subsequently promoted to grade of Brigadier-General, C. S. A., served as Assistant Secretary of State of Confederacy during his administration.

HON. ALEXANDER H. STEPHENS, of Georgia, served as the first and only Vice-President of the Confederate States. As such, he was an ex-officio member of the Confederate Cabinet. He was also, in his Vice-Presidential capacity, President of the Confederate Senate. He served as Vice-President from February 18, 1861, until the downfall of the Confederate Government. He was arrested, by order of the Federal authorities, May 11, 1865.

HON. PHILIP CLAYTON, of Georgia, served as Assistant Secretary of the Confederate Treasury during the greater part of the Confederate War (1861-5) (see Life and Times of C. G. Memminger, first Secretary of the Confederate Treasury, by Henry D. Capers). It is interesting to remember that HON. HENRY D. CAPERS, of Georgia, was appointed and commissioned as Chief Clerk and Disbursing Officer of Treasury Department, C. S. A., February 19, 1861. He served as such for some months (as the records seem to show), becoming, later, Major and Lieutenant-Colonel of Twelfth Georgia Artillery Battalion. He has (I believe) the unique credit of being the oldest commissioned Cabinet Officer of the Confederate Government. HON. BOLLING BAKER, of Georgia, became the First Auditor of the Confederate Treasury. He served, apparently, during the life of the Confederate Government. HON. A. H. (J. A.?) CRAWFORD, of Georgia, was appointed Chief of Bureau of Warrants, Treasury Department, C. S. A., February 22, 1861.

GEN. ALEXANDER R. LAWTON, of Georgia, was the second Quartermaster-General of the Confederacy, he serving from

August 10, 1863, until the close of the War. He was connected with Confederate Department of War, as was also Gen. Isaac M. St. John, of Georgiaa, who was appointed second commissary-general of the Confederacy, Feb. 16, 1865. He served as such, as the records seem to show, until the end of the War.

HON. G. E. W. NELSON, of Georgia, was given the position of Superintendent of Public Printing, C. S. A. He was identified with the Department of Justice.

HON. BENJAMIN H. HILL, of Georgia, was, during the life of the Confederacy, the confidential adviser of President Davis, and of the Confederate Cabinet, on all State questions.

CAMPAIGNS CONDUCTED, AND BATTLES, EN-GAGEMENTS, SKIRMISHES, ETC., FOUGHT WITHIN THE LIMITS OF THE STATE OF GEORGIA, WITH DATES AND LOCATION, 1861-1865.

Acworth, Oct. 4, 1864.
Alexander's Bridge, Sept. 18, 1863.
Allatoona, Oct. 5, 1864.
Alpine, Sept. 3, 5, 8, 12, 1863; May —, 1864.
Armuchee Creek, May 15, 1864.
Atlanta, July 22, 23, Aug. 25, Sept. 2, Nov. 6, 9, 1864.
Bear Creek Station, Nov. 16, 1864.
Beaulieu, Fort, Dec. 14-21, 1864.
Atlanta Campaign, May 1-Sept. 8, 1864.
Atlanta & West Point R. R., July 27-31, 1864.
Augusta Arsenal, Jan. 24, 1861.

Bald Hill, July 21, 1864.
Ball's Ferry, Nov. 23-25, 1864.
Barnesville, April 19, 1865.
Big Shanty, June 9, Oct. 3, 1864.
Blue Bird Gap, Sept. 11, 1863.
Brunswick, June 8, 1863.
Brush Mountain, June —, 1864.
Bryan Court House, Dec. 8, 1864.
Buck Creek, Dec. 7, 1864.
Buck Head, July 18, 1864.
Buck Head Church, Nov. 28, 1864.
Buck Head Creek, Nov. 28, Dec. 2, 1864.
Buck Head Station, Nov. 19, 1864.
Burke's Mill, Feb. 18-19, 1864.
Burnt Hickory, May 24, 1864.
Buzzard Roost, Feb. 24-25, 1864; April 23, 1865.
Buzzard Roost Gap, May 8-11, Oct. 13-14, 1864.

Calhoun, May 16, June 10, 1864.
Campbellton, July 28, Sept. 10, 1864.
Camp Creek, Aug. 18, Sept. 30, 1864.
Cartersville, May 20, July 24, Sept. 20, 1864.

Cassville, May 18-19, 24, 1864.
Catlett's Gap, Sept. 15-18, 1863.
Catoosa Platform, Feb. 27, 1864.
Catoosa Springs, May 3, 1864.
Catoosa Station, Feb. 23, 1864.
Cave Spring Road, Oct. 13, 1864.
Chattahoochee Railroad Bridge, Aug. 26-Sept. 1, 1864.
Chattahoochee River, July 5-17, 1864.
Chattooga River, Sept. 12, 1863.
Cheney's Farm, June 22-27, 1864.
Chickamauga, Sept. 19-20, 1863.
Chickamauga Campaign, Aug. 16-Sept. 22, 1863.
Chickamauga Creek, Jan. 30, May 3, 1864.
Clear Creek, July 30, 1864.
Clinton, July 30, Nov. 20, 21-23, 1864.
Columbus, April 16, 17, 1865.
Coosaville Road, Oct. 12-13, 1864.
Coosawattee River, April 1-4, 1865.
Cotton River Bridge, Nov. 16, 1864.
Covington, July 22-24, 1864.
Crow's Valley, Feb. 24-25, 1864.
Cuyler's Plantation, Dec. 9, 1864.
Cypress Swamp, Dec. 7, 1864.

Dallas, May 24, 26-June 1, Oct. 7, 1864.
Dallas Line, May 25-June 5, 1864.
Dalton, Jan. 6, 21-23, Feb. 22-27, May 13, Aug. 14, Oct. 13, Nov 30, Dec. 5, 1864; March 13, 14, 1865.
Darien, June 11, Sept. 22, 1863.
Davisboro, Nov. 28, 1864.
Davis Cross Roads, Sept. 11, 1863.
Davis' House, Sept. 11, 1863.
Dedmon's Trace, April 10, 1864.
Deer Head Cove, March 29-31, 1864.
Dirt Town, Sept. 12, 1863.
Doboy River, Nov. 13-18, 1862.
Double Bridges, April 18, 1865.
Dry Valley, Sept. 21, 1863.
Ducktown Road, April 3, 1864.
Dug Gap, Sept. 11, 1863; May 8-11, 1864.
Dyer's Ford, Sept. 18, 1863.

East Macon, Nov. 20, 1864.
East Point, Aug. 30, Nov. 15, 1864.
East Tennessee and Georgia Railroad, Nov. 24-27, 1863.
Eatonton, Nov. 21, 1864.
Ebenezer Creek, Dec. 8, 1864.
Eden Station, Dec. 9, 1864.

Elba Island, March 7-11, 1862.
Ellidge's Mill, Feb. 18-19, 1864.
Etowah River, May 20, 1864.
Ezra Church, July 28, 1864.

FB

Fairburn, Aug. 15, Oct. 2, 1864.
Flat Creek, Oct. 11-14, 1864.
Flat Rock Bridge, July 28, 1864.
Flat Rock Road, Oct. 2, 1864.
Flint River, Aug. 19, 1864; April 18, 1865.
Flint River Bridge, Aug. 30, 1864.
Floyd's Spring, May 16, 1864.
Frick's Gap, Feb. 25, 26, 1864.

Georgetown, April 17-30, 1865.
Georgia, Jan. 3-26, 1861; Nov. 14-Dec. 31, 1864.
Georgia, Central, Jan. 1-June 30, 1865.
Georgia, Northern, April 7-12, May 3, 1862; Aug. 11-Oct. 19,
    Oct. 20-Dec. 31, 1863; Jan. 1-April 30, May 1-Nov. 13, 1864;
    Nov. 14, 1864; Jan. 23, 1865; Jan. 1-June 30, 1865.
Georgia, Southern, Jan. 1-June 30, 1865.
Georgia Central Railroad Bridge, Nov. —, 1864.
Georgia Central Railroad Station No. 5, Dec. 4, 1864.
Georgia Coast, Aug. 21, 1861-April 11, 1862; April 12,.1862;
    June 11, 1863; June 12-Dec. 31, 1863; Jan. 1-Nov. 13, 1864.
Gilgal Church, June 10-July 3, 1864.
Gordon, Nov. 21, 1864.
Graysville, Sept. 10, Nov. 26, 1863.
Griswoldville, Nov. 20-22, 1864.

Hillsboro, July 30-31, 1864.
Hinesville, Dec. 16, 1864.
Holly Creek, March 1, 1865.
Howell's Ferry, July 5, Oct. 19, 1864.
Hudson Place Salt Works, Sept. 22, 1863.
Huntsville, May 24, 1864.

Isham's Ford, July —, 1864.

Jackson, Fort, Jan. 26, 1861; Dec. 21,·1864.
Jasper, Aug. 14-15, 1864.
Jenks' Bridge, Dec. 7, 1864.
Johnson's Crook, Feb. 10, 1865.
Jonesboro, Aug. 19, 31-Sept. 1, Nov. 15, 1864.
Jug Tavern, Aug. 3, 1864.

Kennesaw Mountain, June 19-25, 1864; June 27, 1864.
Kennesaw Water Tank, Oct. 3, 1864.
Kingston, May 18-19, Nov. 10-11, 1864.
Kolb's Farm, June 22, 1864.

LaFayette, Sept. 10, 13, 14, Dec. 12, 14, 21-23, 1863; April 11-13, 24-25, June 24, Oct. 12, 1864.
LaFayette Road, Sept. 12, 1863.
Lawrenceville, Oct. 27, 1864.
Lay's Ferry, May 15, 1864.
Lee and Gordon's Mills, Sept. 11-13, 16-18, 1863.
Lee's Cross Roads, May 2, 1864.
Leet's Tan Yard, Sept. 12, 1863; March 5, 1864.
Leggett's Hill, July 21, 1864.
Lithonia, July 28, 1864.
Little Ogeechee River, Dec. 4, 5, 1864.
Lookout Church, Sept. 21, 1863.
Lookout Creek, May 3, 1862.
Lookout Mountain, Sept. 9, 1863.
Lost Mountain, June —, Oct. 4-7, 1864.
Louisville, Nov. 29, 30, 1864.
Lovejoy's Station, July 29, Aug. 18-22, Sept. 2-5, Nov. 16, 1864.
Lumpkin County, Sept. 15, 1864.
Lumpkin's Station, Dec. 4, 1864.

McAfee's Cross Roads, June 11, 1864.
McAllister, Fort, June 29, 1862; Jan. 27, Feb. 28, March 9, 1863; Feb. 1, March 3 (1864?), Dec. 13, 1864.
McDonough Road, Oct. 2, Nov. 6, 1864.
McIntosh County, Aug. 2-4, 1864.
McLemore's Cove, Sept. 11, 1863; March 30-April 1, 1864; Feb. 1, 1865.
Macon & Western Railroad, July 27-31, 1864.
Marietta, June 10-July 3, 1864.
Mill Creek Gap, May 8-11, 1864.
Milledgeville, Nov. 23, 1864.
Millen's Grove, Dec. 1, 1864.
Mimm's Mills, April 20, 1865.
Monteith Swamp, Dec. 9, 1864.
Moon's Station, Oct. 4, 1864.
Mulberry Creek, Aug. 3, 1864.

Neal Dow Station, July 4, 1864.
New Hope Church, May 25-June 5, Oct. 5, 1864.
Nickajack Creek, June —, 1864.
Nickajack Gap, March 9, May 7, 1864.
Nickajack Trace, April 23, 1864.
Noonday Creek, June —, 1864.
Northern Georgia, Sept. 29-Nov. 13, 1864.
Noyes' Creek, June —, Oct. 2-3, 1864.

Oconee River, Nov. 23-25, 1864.
Ogeechee Canal, Dec. 9, 1864.

Ogeechee River, Dec. 7, 1864.
Oglethorpe Barracks, Jan. 26, 1861.
Olley's Creek, June —, 1864.
Ossabaw Island, July 3, 1863.
Ossabaw Sound, June 3, 1864.
Owens' Ford, Sept. 17, 1863.

Pace's Ferry, July 5-17, Aug. 26, 1864.
Parker's Cross Roads, May 16, 1864.
Peachtree Creek, July 19, 20, 1864.
Pea Vine Creek, Sept. 10, 1863.
Pea Vine Ridge, Sept. 18, 1863.
Pickens County, July —, 1864.
Pickett's Mills, May 25-June 5, 1864.
Pigeon Mountain, Sept. 15-18, 1863.
Pine Hill, June 6-18 (?), 1864.
Pine Log Creek, May 18, 1864.
Pleasant Hill, April 18, 1865.
Pooler Station, Dec. 9, 1864.
Powder Springs, June —, Oct. 2-3, 1864.
Pulaski, Fort, Jan. 3, 1861; April 10-11, 1862.
Pumpkin Vine Creek, May 25-June 5, 1864.

Red Oak, Aug. 19, 29, 1864.
Reed's Bridge, Sept. 18, 1863.
Resaca, May 14, 1864.
Reynolds' Plantation, Nov. 28, 1864.
Ringgold, Sept. 11, 17, Dec. 5, 13, 1863; Feb. 8, 18, April 27, 1864; March 20, 1865.
Ringgold Gap, Nov. 27, 1863; May 2, 1864.
Rock Spring, Sept. 12, 1863.
Rocky Creek Bridge, April 20, 1865.
Rocky Creek Church, Dec. 2, 1864.
Rocky Face Ridge, Feb. 24-25, May 8-11, 1864.
Rome, April 26-May 3, Sept. 10, 11, 1863; Jan. 25-Feb. 5, May 15, 17, July 11-13, 28-29, Aug. 11-15, Oct. 10-13, 1864.
Rome Cross Roads, May 16, 1864.
Rosedew, Fort, Dec. 14-21, 1864.
Rossville, Sept. 11, 17, 21, Dec. 5, 14, 1863.
Roswell, Sept. 26, 1864.
Rottenwood Creek, July 4, 1864.
Rough and Ready, Nov. 15, 1864.
Rough and Ready Station, Aug. 31, 1864.
Ruff's Mill, July 4, 1864.
Ruff's Station, Oct. 19, 1864.

Salt Springs, Oct. 1, 1864.
Sandersville, Nov. 25, 26, 1864.

Sand Mountain, Oct. 2, 1864.
Sandtown, Aug. 15, 1864.
Savannah, Dec. 10, 11-21, 1864.
Savannah Campaign, Nov. 15-Dec. 21, 1864.
Savannah River, March 7-11, Sept. 30-Oct. 3, 1862.
Shadna Church, Oct. 2, 1864.
Shady Grove, Dec. 1, 1864.
Ship's Gap, Oct. 16, 1864.
Sisters Ferry, Dec. 7, 1864.
Snake Creek Gap, May 8, Sept. 15, Oct. 15, 1864.
Snapfinger Creek, July 27, 1864.
South Newport, Aug. 17, 1864.
South River, July 27-31, Oct. 24, 1864.
Spaulding's, Nov. 7, 1862.
Spring Creek, Sept. 18, 1863.
Springfield, Dec. 10, 1864.
Spring Hill, April 20, 1865.
Spring Place, Feb. 27, April 1-4, 1865.
Statesboro, Dec. 4, 1864.
Station No. 5, Georgia Central Railroad, Dec. 4, 1864.
Stevens' Gap, Sept. 6, 18, 1863; Feb. 25-26, 1864.
Stilesboro, May 23, June 9, 1864.
Stockbridge, Nov. 15, 1864.
Stone Church, Feb. 7, May 1, 1864.
Subligna, Jan. 22, 1864.
Sugar Valley, May 8-13, 1864.
Sulphur Springs, Sept. 2-5, 1864.
Summerville, Sept. 6-7, 10, 13, 15, 1863; May —, Oct. 18, 1864;
    May 5, 1865.
Sweet Water Creek, Oct. 2-3, 1864.
Sylvan Grove, Nov. 27, 1864.

Taylor's Ridge, Nov. 27, 1863; April 14, 27, 1864.
Thomas' Station, Dec. 3, 1864.
Tifton, May 13, Oct. 13, 1864.
Tobesofkee Creek, April 20, 1865.
Towaliga Bridge, Nov. 17, 1864.
Trenton, Aug. 28-31, Nov. 18, 1863.
Trickum's Cross Roads, Oct. 26-29, 1864.
Trion Factory, Sept. 15, 1863.
Tunnel Hill, Sept. 11, 1863; Feb. 23, 24, April 29, May 2, 5-7,
    1864; March 3, 1865.
Turner's Ferry, July 5-17, Aug. 26, Oct. 19, 1864.
Tybee Island, Nov. 24, 1861.
Tyler, Fort, April 16, 1865.

Utoy Creek, Aug. 6, 1864.

Van Wert, Oct. 9-10, 1864.
Varnell's Station, May 7, 9, 12, 1864.
Varnell's Station Road, May 4, 1864.
Venus Point, Feb. 15, 1862.
Vernon River, Dec. 15-21, 1864.

Walnut Creek, Nov. 20, 1864.
Warsaw Sound, June 17, 1863.
Watkins' Ferry, May 3, 1862.
Waynesboro, Nov. 27-28, Dec. 4, 1864.
Westbrook's, Oct. 2, 1864.
West Point, April 16, 1865.
Whitemarsh Island, March 30-31, April 16, 1862; Feb. 22, 1864.
Wilmington Island, March 30-31, 1862.
Wilmington Narrows, Jan. 26-28, 1862.

ROLL OF HONOR.

General Orders No. 131.
Adjutant and Inspector General's Office,
Richmond, Va., October 3, 1863.

Difficulties in procuring the medals and badges of distinction having delayed their presentation by the President, as authorized by the act of Congress approved October 13, 1862, to the officers, non-commissioned officers and privates of the armies of the Confederate States conspicuous for courage and good conduct on the field of battle, to avoid postponing the grateful recognition of their valor until it can be made in the enduring form provided by that Act, it is ordered:

I. That the names of all those who have been, or may hereafter be, reported as worthy of this distinction be inscribed on a roll of honor, to be preserved in the office of the Adjutant and Inspector General for reference in all future time, for those who have deserved well of their country, as having best displayed their courage and devotion on the field of battle.

II. That the Roll of Honor, as far as now made up, be appended to this Order and read at the head of every regiment in the service of the Confederate States at the first dress-parade after its receipt and be published in at least one newspaper in each State.

III. The attention of the officers in charge is directed to General Orders No. 93, Section 27, of the services of 1862, Adjutant and Inspector General's Office, for mode of selecting the non-commissioned officers and privates entitled to this distinction and its execution is enjoined.

By Order.

, S. Cooper,
Adjutant and Inspector General.

General Orders No. 64.
Adjutant and Inspector General's Office.
Richmond, Va., August 10, 1864.

I. The following Roll of Honor is published in accordance with paragraph 1, General Orders No. 131, 1863. It will be read to every regiment in service at the first dress-parade after its receipt.

Names of Officers Killed or Who Died of Wounds not Mentioned in the Formal Reports.

GEORGIA.

1st Infantry (Regulars), Captain John G. Patton, Lieutenant H. J. Porter and Crawford Tucker, killed August 30.

7th Infantry, Captain D. F. Peek and Lieutenant W. M. Delk, died of wounds received August 30. Lieutenant A. Y. White, killed August 30.

8th Infantry, Captains J. M. C. Husley and Jacob Phinizy, killed August 30.

11th Infantry, Captain E. W. Jackson, Lieutenants George S. Burson and John B. Buerry, killed August 30.

12th Infantry, Lieutenant John T. Chambliss, killed August 9th.

14th Infantry, Captain R. W. McMichael, killed August 29.

15th Infantry, Lieutenants James M. Carson and J. L. Cunning, killed August 30.

19th Infantry, Lieutenant F. A. Wilde, killed August 31.

22d Infantry, Captain J. T. Albert and Lieutenant S. M. Smith, killed August 30.

45th Infantry, Captain Joseph H. White, died of wounds received August 29; R. W. Brown died of wounds received August 9.

48th Infantry, Captain Allen Kelly, killed August 29.

49th Infantry, J. W. Gainer, killed August 29.

Battle of Chancellorsville.

GEORGIA.

Fourth Regiment of Infantry:
    Private W. Sparks, Co. A.
    Sergeant Hill M. Taylor, Co. B.
    Color Corporal John T. Moore, Go. C.
    The other companies declined making selections.
Fourteenth Regiment of Infantry:
    Lieutenant Colonel J. M. Fielder.
    Captain T. T. Mounger.
    Captain R. P. Harman.

First Lieutenant H. A. Soloman.
Private Daniel Kennington, Co. B.
Corporal William M. Tomlinson, Co. C.
Corporal Joseph G. Dupree, Co. D.
Second Sergeant Thomas D. Smith, Co. H.
Private James F. D. Thaxton, Co. I.
Private James M. Brock, Co. K.
The other companies declined making selections.
Twelfth Regiment of Infantry:
First Lieutenant Thomas W. Harris, Co. C.
Second Lieutenant J. A. Walker, Co. B.
Second Lieutenant W. F. Lowe, Co. F.
Private J. L. Batts, Co. A.
Private Abel James, Co. B.
Private S. M. Beavers, Co. C.
Private W. W. Forrester, Co. D.
Private R. J. Orr, Co. E.
First Sergeant N. M. Howard, Co. F.
Private James M. Bullard, Co. G.
Private Archibald McDonald, Co. H.
First Sergeant B. L. Stephens, Co. I.
Private W. H. Burgamy, Co. K.
Thirty-Fifth Regiment of Infantry:
Corporal Jackson Baggett, Co. A.
Private A. S. W. Bass, Co. B.
Second Sergeant J. A. Cochran, Co. C.
Private Rolla Willingham, Co. D.
Private D. P. White, Co. E.
Private R. D. B. Holt, Co. F.
Private W. E. Moore, Co. G.
Private Absalom Martin, Co. H.
Private Lewis (J.) Millican, Co. I.
Private D. M. Pearce, Co. K.
Forty-Fourth Regiment of Infantry:
Private James Fambrough, Co. C.
Private James A. McNatt, Co. F.
The other companies declined making selections.
Forty-Fifth Regiment of Infantry:
Captain William H. Shaw, Co. A.
Private John D. Pate, Co. A.
Private John H. King, Co. C.
Private James M. Lawrence, Co. E.
Private James P. Green, Co. F.
Private John S. Bonner, Co. G.
Private H. W. Dent, Co. H.
Private W. W. Wilson, Co. I.

Private M. H. Fitzpatrick, Co. K.
Company B declined making selections.
Forty-Ninth Regiment of Infantry:
Sergeant H. A. Hall, Co. A.
Private Lewis White, Co. B.
Sergeant (A) M. Watkins, Co. C.
Sergeant W. T. Moore, Co. D.
Corporal James (V) Hollingworth, Co. E.
Corporal L. D. Taylor, Co. F.
Corporal J. N. Jordan, Co. G.
Private Joseph Bell, Co. H.
Private F. B. Poole, Co. I.
Private James Taylor, Co. K.
Twenty-First Regiment of Infantry:
Declined making selections.

Battle of Chickamauga.

GEORGIA.

Fifth Regiment of Infantry:
Private J. Kirby Brown, Co. A.
Private Thomas P. Weir, Co. B.
Corporal John Fox, Co. C.
Private James W. Hall, Co. D.
Corporal John B. Johnson, Co. E.
Company H made no selection.
Private William M. Blackwell, Co. F.
Private T. H. Devane, Co. G.
First Sergeant John P. Chapman, Co. I.
Private James Torrence, Co. K.

Battle Near Petersburg, Virginia.

GEORGIA.

Third Regiment Georgia Infantry:
Corporal F. J. Herndon, Co. F.

Battle of Murfreesborough.

GEORGIA.

Fifth Regiment of Infantry:
Private Newton Rice, Co. A.
Corporal Michael McNamara, Co. C.
Private Thomas J. Brantley, Co. E.
Sergeant Samuel P. Kiddoo, Co. F.

129

Corporal B. D. Bedell, Co. H.
Private George W. Horsley, Co. K.
Third Battalion of Infantry:
Private A. S. Kimrey, Co. B.
Private W. D. Clark, Co. C.
Private Mathew Hall, Co. D.
Private John Capps, Co. E.
Ninth Battalion of Infantry:
Private Obey McCarry, Co. A.
Private W. J. Wood, Co. B.
Private N. W. Rice, Co. C.
Private Michael Kinney, Co. F.
Private Thomas Nolan, Co. G.
Private G. W. Sanders, Co. H.
Corporal William M. Gaines, Co. D.
Private C. M. R. Palmer, Co. E.

Battle of Gettysburg.

GEORGIA.

Cobb's Legion:
Sergeant J. L. Born, Co. C.
Sergeant A. C. Adair, Co. D.
Phillips' Legion:
Private Alfred Norris, Co. E.
Private E. J. Smith, Co. E.
Private Thomas B. Jolly, Co. B.
Corporal James D. Putman, Co. F.
Private Michael McGovern, Co. F.
Private J. A. Blanton, Co. B.
Private Ootero (?), Co. D.

"THE WAR OF THE REBELLION.

OFFICIAL RECORDS OF THE UNION AND CONFEDERATE ARMIES.

Series 1st, Vol. XXI, pp. 578 and 582.

Operations in Virginia, West Virginia, Maryland and

Pennsylvania.

No. 271.

Report of Major-General Lafayette McLaws, C. S. Army, commanding McLaws' Division:

Headquarters Division, Camp near Fredericksburg, Va., Dec. 30, 1862:

My aide-de-camp, Captain H. L. P. King, was killed on

Marye's Hill, pierced with five balls, while conveying an order to Brigadier-General Cobb. He was a brave and accomplished officer and gentleman, and had already distinguished himself during the operations in front of Fredericksburg, as he had done in all the other engagements when on duty."

NOTE.—The following members of the Georgia Hussars—a Savannah command—which constituted Company F of the Jeff Davis Mississippi Legion, are mentioned on the Roll of Honor, as published by General Samuel Cooper, Adjutant and Inspector-General, C. S. A., Richmond, Va., December 10, 1864, in connection with the Battle of Upperville, Va., June 21, 1863, and miscellaneous engagements: Captain David Waldhauer, 2d Lieutenant W. W. Gordon, 2d Lieutenant J. McL. Turner, Sergeant L. H. Clemens, Sergeant M. G. Prendergast, and Privates G. N. Saussy, William Lake, F. Bird, C. H. Mann, William Frew and J. (T.?) H. Lake.

VOLUNTEER FORCE OF THE UNITED STATES ARMY FROM GEORGIA, 1861-1865.

FIRST INFANTRY BATTALION.

(This battalion, composed of two companies, was organized at Marietta, Ga., October 31, 1864, to serve three years. It was mustered out of service July 19, 1865, in accordance with orders from the War Department.)

Captain, Alonzo M. Rogers, appointed October 31, 1864.

First lieutenant, Porter T. Southworth, appointed October 31, 1864.

Second lieutenant, William B. Waring, appointed March 17, 1865.

CASUALTIES.

LOCAL DESIGNATIONS OF GEORGIA TROOPS IN THE CONFEDERATE ARMY.

Acworth Grays (Company C, 7th Georgia State Guards).
Albany Guards (Company E, 4th Georgia Infantry).
Alexander Cavalry (Company —, Local Defense Troops, Georgia).
Allapaha Guards (Company E, 29th Georgia Infantry).
Allapaha Rangers (Company —, in N. A. Carswell's Battalion, 22d Georgia State Guards).
Allen Rangers (Company —, Local Defense Troops, Georgia).
Alpharetta Infantry (Company F, 8th Georgia State Guards).
Altamaha Scouts (Company F, 25th Georgia Infantry).
Americus Volunteers (Company K, 9th Georgia Infantry).
Anderson Guards (Six Months Local Defense Troops, Georgia).
Anthony Greys (Company A, 60th Georgia Infantry).
Appling Cavalry (Six Months' Local Defense Troops, Georgia).
Arnett Rifles (Company I, 31st· Georgia Infantry).
Athens Guards (Company —, 3rd Georgia Infantry).
Athens Reserve Corps (Local Defense Troops, Georgia).
Atlanta Arsenal Battery (Captain C. C. Campbell's Company, Georgia Artillery).
Atlanta Fire Company No. 1 (Company A, Atlanta Fire Battalion, Georgia).
Atlanta Greys (Company L, 1st Georgia Regulars).
Atlanta Greys (Company F, 8th Georgia Infantry).
Atlanta Press Guard (Company H, Atlanta Fire Battalion, Georgia).
Atlanta Scouts (Company —, — Georgia Volunteers).
Atlanta Volunteers (Company —, — Georgia Volunteers).
Atlantic and Gulf Guards (Company A, 3d Battalion (Clinch's) Georgia Cavalry, afterward Company G, 4th Georgia (Clinch's) Cavalry).
Augusta Guards (Captain W. C. Dillon's Company, Georgia Volunteers).
Augusta Volunteer Artillery (Captain G. T. Barnes' Company Georgia Artillery).
Bailey Volunteers (Company B, 30th Georgia Infantry).
Bainbridge Independents (Company G, 1st Georgia Infantry).
Baker Fire Eaters (Company H, 6th Georgia Infantry).
Baker Volunteers (Company G, 3d Battalion, Georgia Infantry).

Baldwin Blues (Company H, 4th Georgia Infantry).

Baldwin Cavalry (Company C, Linton Stephens' Battalion, Local Defense Troops, Georgia).

Baldwin Infantry (Captain J. N. Moore's Company, Six Months Local Defense Troops, Georgia).

Baldwin Volunteers (Company F, 9th Georgia Infantry).

Banks County Guards (Company A, 2d Georgia Infantry).

Banks Rifles (Captain Hardy's Company, Georgia Volunteers).

Bartow Artillery (Originally Company A, 4th Battalion Georgia Infantry; afterward Company A, 60th Georgia Infantry; afterward Company A, 22d Battalion, Georgia Siege Artillery).

Bartow Avengers (Company K, 21st Georgia Infantry).

Bartow Avengers (Company E, 60th Georgia Infantry).

Bartow Avengers (Company B, 35th Georgia Infantry).

Bartow Home Guards (Company H, 4th Georgia Reserves).

Bartow Invincibles (Company H, 23d Georgia Infantry).

Bartow Invincibles (Company E, 30th Georgia Infantry).

Bartow Light Infantry (13th Georgia Volunteers).

Bartow Light Infantry (Company G, 26th Georgia Infantry).

Bartow Raid Repellers (Company C, 9th Battalion, Georgia State Guards).

Bartow Yankee Killers (Company A, 23d Georgia Infantry).

Battle Ground Guards (Company F, 48th Georgia Infantry).

Beauregard Rifles (Company C, 6th Georgia Infantry).

Beauregard Volunteers (Company C, 6th Georgia Infantry).

Bell Rangers (Company E, 19th Battalion, Georgia Infantry).

Beman Mounted Infantry (Company E, Linton Stephens' Battalion, Local Defense Troops, Georgia).

Ben Gilham Rangers (Company D, 9th Georgia State Guards).

Ben Hill Infantry (Company F, 21st Georgia Infantry).

Benjamin Infantry (Company E, 10th Georgia Infantry).

Ben Minor Dragoons (Company E, 2d Georgia Cavalry).

Berrien Cavalry (Company F, 11th Georgia State Guards).

Berrien County Light Infantry (Company I, 50th Georgia Infantry).

Berrien Minute Men (Company C, afterward 29th Georgia Infantry).

Berry Infantry (Company I, 29th Georgia Infantry).

Bibb Greys (Company —, 21st Georgia Infantry).

Bibb Volunteer Guards (Captain H. L. Jewett's Company of the Macon Battalion, Local Defense Troops, Georgia).

Big Spring Cavalry (Captain J. M. Denman's Independent Company, Georgia Cavalry).

Big Spring Volunteers (Captain Joshua McConnell's Company, Georgia Volunteers).

Black Creek Volunteers (Company G, 25th Georgia Infantry).

Blodget Artillery (Originally Company I, 3d Georgia Infantry; afterward Captain Foster Blodget's Company, Georgia Artillery).

Blodget Volunteers (Originally Company I, 3d Georgia Infantry; afterward Captain Foster Blodget's Company, Georgia Artillery).

Blood Mountain Tigers (Company F, Colonel S. J. Smith's partisan rangers, Georgia Cavalry).

Blue Caps Cavalry (Company E, 2d Battalion, Georgia Cavalry; afterward Company C, 5th Georgia Cavalry).

Blue Cap Cavalry Troop (Company E, 2d Battalion, Georgia Cavalry, afterward Company C, 5th Georgia Cavalry).

Blue Ridge Guards (Captain N. F. Howard's Company, Georgia Volunteers).

Blue Ridge Tiger Regiment (Also called Banks' Troopers).

Brown Mounted Riflemen (4th Georgia State Guards).

Border Rangers (Company I, 5th Georgia Cavalry).

Border Rangers (Company B, 20th Georgia Infantry).

Bowdon Volunteers (Company B, Cobb's Legion, Georgia Cavalry).

Bragg Rifles (20th Georgia Infantry).

Breckinridge Cavalry (Company F, McDonald's Battalion; Local Defense Troops, Georgia).

Brooks Cavalry (Company D, 11th Georgia State Guards).

Brooks Rifles (Company C, 26th Georgia Infantry).

Brooks Rifles (Company H, 9th Georgia Infantry).

Brooks Volunteers (Company K, 50th Georgia Infantry).

Brown Guards (Company A, Linton Stephens' Battalion, Local Defense Troops, Georgia).

Brown Infantry (Company C, 1st Confederate Georgia Infantry).

Brown Light Infantry (Company C, 25th Georgia Infantry).

Brown Light Infantry (Company F, 25th Georgia Infantry).

Brown Rifles (Company F, 3d Georgia Infantry).

Brunswick Defenders (Company G, 1st Georgia Regulars).

Brunswick Riflemen (Company K, 26th Georgia Infantry).

Bryan Guards (Company D, 25th Georgia Infantry).

Bryan Independent Riflemen (Company A, 25th Georgia Infantry).

Bryan Independent Rifles (Company B, 25th Georgia Infantry).

Buena Vista Cavalry (Captain Brett's Company, Georgia Volunteers).

Buena Vista Guards (Company I, 2d Georgia Infantry).

Bullard Guards (Company D, 59th Georgia Infantry).

Bulloch Guards (Company C, 47th Georgia Infantry).

Bulloch Troop (Company C, 2d Battalion, Georgia Cavalry).
Burke Guards (3d Georgia Infantry).
Burke Volunteers (Company D, 48th Georgia Infantry).
Butler Van-Guard (Company G, 6th Georgia Infantry).
Butts Avengers (Company B, 7th Georgia State Guards).
Butts County Volunteers (Volunteers Company D, 6th Georgia Infantry).
Butts Invincibles (Company A, 30th Georgia Infantry).
Calhoun Cavalry (Captain W. J. Reeves' Company, Georgia State Guards).
Calhoun County Cavalry (Captain C. M. Davis' Company, T. R. Stewart's Battalion, Local Defense Troops, Georgia).
Calhoun Guards (Company D, 12th Georgia Infantry).
Calhoun Rifles (Company D, 12th Georgia Infantry).
Calhoun Repeaters (On register Company I, (L) on rolls Company H, afterward Company C, 25th Georgia Infantry).
Camden Mounted Rifles (Company C, 4th Georgia Cavalry (Clinch's).
Camden Rifles (Company B, 26th Georgia Infantry).
Campbell Greys (Company G, 30th Georgia Infantry).
Campbell Guards (Company A, 3d Battalion, Georgia Infantry; afterward Company A, 21st Georgia Infantry).
Campbell Sharpshooters (Company F, 30th Georgia Infantry).
Campbell Siege Artillery (Captain Charles, G. Campbell's Company, Georgia Artillery).
Campbell Volunteers (Company E, 35th Georgia Infantry).
Canton Infantry (Company B, Cherokee Legion, Georgia Volunteers).
Carroll Cavalry (Company D, 10th Georgia State Guards).
Carroll Guards (Company I, 10th Georgia State Guards).
Carroll Infantry (Company I, 7th Georgia State Guards).
Caswell Guards (Company —, 3d Georgia Infantry).
Catoosa Infantry (Company B, 1st Battalion, Georgia Infantry).
Cave Spring (Mounted Infantry) (Company B, Floyd Legion, Georgia State Guards).
Cedartown Guards (Company D, 21st Georgia Infantry).
Central City Blues (Company H, 12th Georgia Infantry).
Centre Hill Guards (Company —, — Georgia Volunteers).
Chatham Artillery (Captain Joseph S. Claghorn's Company, Georgia Artillery; detached from 1st Georgia Volunteers).
Chatham Light Horse (Company F, 2d Battalion, Georgia Cavalry).
Chatham Siege Artillery (Companies A and B, Battalion Georgia Artillery).
Chatham Volunteers (Company E, 47th Georgia Infantry).
Chattahoochee Beauregards (Company C, 10th Georgia Infantry).

Chattahoochee Cavalry (Company —, 4th Georgia State Guards) (Blue Ridge Tiger Regiment).

Chattahoochee Defenders (Company E, 5h Georgia State Guards).

Chattahoochee Guard (Company I, 5th Georgia State Guards).

Chattahoochee Rifles (Captain H. A. Pratt's Company, Georgia ——).

Chattahoochee Volunteers (Company K, 30th Georgia Infantry).

Chattanooga Cavalry (Company G, Culberson's Battalion, Local Defense Troops, Georgia).

Chattooga Volunteers (Company —, — Georgia —).

Cherokee Brown Riflemen (Company —, — Georgia —).

Cherokee Cavalry (Company B, Phillip's Legion, Georgia Volunteers).

Cherokee Georgia Mountaineers (Company F, 28th Georgia Infantry).

Cherokee Home Guards—Infantry—(Company C, Cherokee Legion, Georgia).

Cherokee Lincoln Killers—Cavalry—(Company C, Cherokee Legion, Georgia).

Cherokee Rangers (Company F, 3d Georgia Cavalry).

Cherokee Rangers—Cavalry—(Company A, Cherokee Legion, Georgia).

Cherokee Repellers—Infantry—(Company D, Cherokee Legion, Georgia).

Cherokee Revengers—Infantry—(Company A, Cherokee Legion, Georgia).

Cherokee Stone-Walls—Infantry—(Company G, Cherokee Legion, Georgia).

Cherokee Volunteers—Infantry—(Company E, Cherokee Legion, Georgia).

Chesatee Artillery (Captain Thomas H. Bomar's Company, Georgia Artillery; originally Company N, 38th Georgia Infantry).

Chulio Guards (Chulio Mounted Infantry) (Company F, Floyd Legion, Georgia State Guards).

Citizen Infantry (Company F, Fire Battalion, Augusta, Georgia).

City Guard (Augusta, Georgia).

City Guards (Company C, 5th Georgia State Guards).

Clarke County Guards (Company G, 9th Georgia State Guards).

Clarke County Light Artillery (Captain Franklin Roberts' Company, Arkansas Artillery; temporarily attached as Company E, 14th Battalion, Georgia Artillery).

Clay Volunteers (Captain Isham Wood's Company, T. R. Stewart's Battalion, Local Defense Troops, Georgia).

Clay Volunteers (Company I, 51st Georgia Infantry).

Clayton Dragoons (Company F, 2d Georgia Cavalry).

Clayton Invincibles (Company I, 30th Georgia Infantry).

Clinch Cavaliers (Company G, 11th Georgia State Guards).

Clinch Rangers (—, — Georgia).

Clinch Rifles (Company A, 5th Georgia Infantry).

Clinch Volunteers (Company G, 50th Georgia Infantry).

Clinton Guards (Company B, 6th Georgia State Guards).

Coast Rifles (Company F, 1st Volunteers, Georgia Infantry).

Cobb Chattahoochee Volunteers (Company L, 7th Georgia State Guards).

Cobb Guards (Company D, 3d Georgia Reserves).

Cobb Guards (Company A. Company G, 22d Battalion, Georgia Artillery; temporarily attached).

Cobb Guards (Company B, Company H, 22d Battalion, Georgia Artillery; temporarily attached).

Cobb Invincibles (Company F, Cobb's Legion, Georgia Volunteers)

Cobb Repellers (Company K, 7th Georgia State Guards).

Cobb's Infantry (Company E, 16th Georgia Infantry).

Cobb's Legion (Georgia Volunteers)

Coffee Guards (Company C, 50th Georgia Infantry).

Coffee Revengers (Captain D. Newbern's Company, Six Months' Local Defense Troops, Georgia).

Cold Water Guards (Rebels) (Company E, 34th Georgia Infantry).

Cold Steel Guards (Company H, 49th Georgia Infantry).

Colquitt Home Guards (— Georgia Volunteers).

Colquitt Marksmen (Company H, 50th Georgia Infantry).

Columbus City Light Guard (Company A, 2d Independent Battalion, Georgia Infantry).

Columbus Guards (Company G, 2d Georgia Infantry).

Columbus Light Artillery (Captain E. Croft's Independent Company, Georgia Artillery).

Company "B" (Company D, 5th Georgia State Guards).

Confederate Continentals (Company —, O — Georgia).

Confederate Guards (Company A, 13th Georgia Infantry).

Confederate Invincibles (20th Georgia Volunteers).

Confederate Light Guards (Company G, 3d Georgia Infantry).

Confederate Sentinels (Company F, 20th Georgia Infantry).

Confederate States Sentinels (Company A, 10th Georgia Infantry).

Cotton Planters Guards (Company E, 59th Georgia Infantry).

Covington Infantry (Company I, 8th Georgia State Guards).

Cow Hunters (Also called Irwin Cow Boys,—Company A 7th Georgia Infantry).

Coweta Second District Guards (Company A, 7th Georgia Infantry).

Coweta Volunteers (Company H, 7th Georgia State Guards).

Crawford Greys (Company E, 6th Georgia Infantry).

Crawford Rangers (20th Georgia Infantry).

Crawford Rifles (Captain D. Kirkpatrick, Jr.'s Company, Georgia Volunteers).

Culpeper Hussars (Company F, Stephens' Battalion, Georgia State Guards).

Dabney Rifles (Company G, 21st Georgia Infantry).

Dade Rifles (Company K, 3d Georgia State Troops).

Dahlonega Volunteers (Company H, 1st Georgia Volunteers).

Dalton Home Guard (Company H, 1st Georgia State Guards).

Dalton Machinery Guards (Captain J. H. Bard's Company, Six Months' Local Defense Troops, Georgia).

Davis Guards (Company F, 12th Georgia Infantry).

Davis Infantry (Company K, 7th Georgia Infantry).

Davis Musketeers (Company K, 10th Georgia Infantry).

Davis Rifles (Company C, 12th Georgia Infantry).

Dawson County Independents (Company I, 22d Georgia Infantry).

Dawson Greys (Company C, 3d Georgia Infantry).

Dawson Volunteers (Company E, 5th Georgia Infantry).

Decatur Cavalry (Company I, 11th Georgia State Guards).

Decatur Grays (Company D, 17th Georgia Infantry).

Decatur Infantry (Company F, 50th Georgia Infantry).

Decatur Infantry (Captain R. Sims' Company, attached to 6th Georgia State Guards).

De Kalb Cavalry (Company A, 10th Georgia State Guards).

De Kalb Guards (Company D, 61st Georgia Infantry).

De Kalb Guards (Company B, 26th Georgia Infantry).

De Kalb Murphy Guards (Also called Murphy Guards) (Company C, afterward A, 38th Georgia Infantry).

De Kalb Silver Greys (Company B, 8th Georgia State Guards).

Delhi Rangers (Company A, 15th Georgia Infantry).

Dick Davis Guards (Company A, 9th Georgia State Guards).

Dillard Rangers (Company A, 3d Georgia Cavalry).

District Town Calvary (Captain J. Jones' Company, F. Culberson's Battalion, Local Defense Troops, Georgia).

Dixie Rangers (Company C, 65th Georgia Infantry).

Dooly Guards (Company G, 60th Georgia Infantry).

Dooly Volunteers (Captain J. D. Wilkes' Company, Wilson's Battalion, Local Defense Troops, Georgia).

Dougherty Greys (Company —, 51st Georgia Infantry).

Dougherty Guards (Company K, 51st Georgia Infantry).

Dougherty Hussars (Company D, Cobb's Legion, afterward 9th Georgia Cavalry, Georgia Volunteers).

Douglass Guards (Captain E. L. Douglass's Company, Yarborough's Battalion, Local Defense Troops, Georgia).

Eagle Guards (Companies A and B, Thompson's Battalion, Local Defense Troops, Georgia).

Early Dragoons (Captain T. T. Swann's Company, Stewartt's Cavalry Battalion, Local Defense Troops, Georgia).

Early Guards (Company G, 13th Georgia Infantry).

Early Volunteers (Company A, 51st Georgia Infantry).

Echols Cavalry (Company E, 11th Georgia State Guards).

Echols Guards (Company D, 8th Georgia Infantry).

Echols Light Artillery (Captain John H. Tiller's Company, Georgia Artillery).

Effingham Hussars (Company A. 2d Battalion, Georgia Cavalry).

Effingham Minute Men (Captain A. P. Longstreet's Company, Wright's Battalion. Local Defense Troops, Georgia).

Elbert Volunteers (Company H. 3d Georgia State Guards).

Emanuel Rangers (Company —, 20th Georgia Infantry).

Emmett Rifles (Originally Company C. 1st Volunteers, Georgia Infantry; afterward Company F. 22d Battalion, Georgia Siege Artillery).

Emmett Rifles (Company B, 1st Georgia Regulars).

Empire State Guards (Company I, 47th Georgia Infantry).

Etowah Invincibles (Captain Thomas M. Compton's Company, Georgia Infantry).

Evans Guards (Company K, 13th Georgia Infantry).

Factory Guards (Captain W. H. Amason's Company, Macon Battalion, Local Defense Troops, Georgia).

Fannin Guards (Company B, 4th Battalion, afterward 60th Regiment, Georgia Infantry).

FanninVolunteers (Captain James Kincaid's Company, Gilmer Battalion, Local Defense Troops, Georgia).

Faulk Invincibles (Company E, 26th Georgia Infantry).

Fayette Grey Guards (Company I, 10th Georgia Infantry).

Fayetteville Rifle Greys (Company I, 10th Georgia Infantry).

Fayette Rangers (Company F, 13th Georgia Infantry).

Fayette Volunteers (Company H, 30th Georgia Infantry).

Firemen Guards (Captain G. S. Oberas' Company, Macon Battalion, Local Defense Troops, Georgia).

Fireside Rangers (Company C, 15th Georgia Infantry).

Flint Cavalry (Company K, 11th Georgia State Guards).

Floyd Cavalry (Company E, Floyd Legion, Georgia Volunteers).

Floyd Infantry (Company H, 8th Georgia Infantry).

Floyd Legion (Georgia Volunteers).

Floyd Rangers (Company D, Floyd Legion Georgia Volunteers).

Floyd Rifles (Company C, 2d Independent Battalion, Georgia Infantry).

Floyd Rifles (Company A, Macon Battalion, Local Defense Troops, Georgia).

Floyd Sharpshooters (Company B, 21st Georgia Infantry).

Floyd Springs Guards (Company C, 23d Georgia Infantry).

Floyd's Newton Cavalry (Company K, 10th Georgia State Guards).

Forrest's Artillery (Capt. C. O. Stillwell's Company, (I) Floyd Legion, Georgia State Troops).

Forest City Rangers (Captain C. H. Way's Company, Georgia Volunteers).

Forrest Rangers (Company H, 26th Georgia Infantry).

Forsyth Chattahoochee Cavalry (Company —, Blue Ridge Tiger Regiment, 4th Georgia State Guards).

Forsyth Mounted Greys (Company K, Cherokee Legion, Georgia Infantry).

Forsyth Mounted Guards (Company K, Cherokee Legion, Georgia Infantry).

Fort Gaines Guards (Company D, 9th Georgia Infantry).

Fort Valley Cavalry (Company —, 12th Georgia State Guards).

Franklin County Guards (Captain S. W. Kay's Company, Six Months' Local Defense Troops, Georgia).

Franklin County Reserves (Company C, Whitehead's Battalion, Local Defense Troops, Georgia).

Freeman Guards (Company G, 28th Georgia Infantry).

F. S. Slaters (Company —, — Georgia —).

Fulton Dragoons (Company G, Cobb's Legion, Georgia Volunteers).

Gainesville Light Infantry (Company A, 11th Georgia Infantry).

Gardner Volunteers (Company H, 22d Georgia Infantry).

Garrison Guards Battalion (1st Regiment, Georgia State Line).

Georgia Dragoons (Company G, 2d Georgia Cavalry).

Georgia Defenders (Captain F. S. Chapman's Independent Company, Georgia State Troops).

Georgia Coast Rifles (Company F, 1st Volunteers, Georgia Infantry).

Georgia Dragoons (Company E, 4th (Avery's) Georgia Cavalry).

Georgia Mounted Dragoons (Company I, 4th (Avery's) Georgia Cavalry).

Georgia Fire Company (Company E, Augusta Fire Battalion Local Defense Troops, Georgia).

Georgia Forresters (Company F, 29th Georgia Infantry).

Georgia Guards (Company F, 6th Georgia Guards).

Georgia Hussars (Company A, Captain J. F. Waring's Independent Georgia Company; assigned October 14, 1861 as

141

Company E, 6th Virginia Cavalry; relieved and assigned as Company F, Jeff Davis Legion, December 7, 1861).

Georgia Hussars (Company B, Captain W. H. Wiltberger, Company D, 2d Battalion, Georgia Cavalry).

Georgia Light Artillery (Captain Horatio N. Hollifield's Company, State Troops).

Georgia Light Infantry (Company A, 31st Georgia Infantry).

Georgia Rangers (Company G, 10th Georgia Infantry).

Georgia Rangers (62d Georgia Cavalry).

Georgia Regulars (See Hamilton Battery).

Georgia Troopers (Company C, 9th Georgia Cavalry).

Georgia Troopers (Company H, 9th Georgia Cavalry).

Georgia Volunteers (Company H, 2d Georgia Infantry).

German Volunteers (Company I, 1st Georgia Volunteers).

Gibson Guards (Company A, 48th Georgia Infantry).

Gilmer Battalion (Local Defense Troops, Georgia).

Gilmer Blues (Company K, 6th Georgia Infantry).

Gilmer Guards (Captain D. M. West's Company, Gilmer Battalion, Local Defense Troops, Georgia).

Gilmer Light Guards (Company B, Smith's Legion, Georgia Volunteers; afterward Company A, 65th Georgia Infantry).

Gilmer Rifles (Captain John E. Mitchell's Company, Jackson's Regiment, Georgia Volunteers).

Gilmer Volunteers (Company F, 60th Georgia Infantry).

Glascock Rangers (Captain R. Walden's Company, Stephens' Battalion, Local Defense Troops, Georgia).

Glover Guards (Company G, 4th Georgia Infantry).

Glynn Guards (Company A, 26th Georgia Infantry).

Glynn Guards (Company B, 4th (Clinch's) Georgia Cavalry).

Goshen Blues (Company H, 38th Georgia Infantry).

Governor's Guard (Company E, 3d Georgia Infantry).

Governor's Horse Guards (Company A, Cavalry Battalion, Phillips' Legion, Georgia).

Grant Factory Guards (Captain J. J. Grant's Company, Thompson's Battalion, Local Defense Troops, Georgia).

Gresham Rifles (Company, A, 45th Georgia Infantry).

Griffin Light Artillery (Captain O. C. Gibson's Company, Georgia Artillery).

Griffin Light Guards (Company B, 5th Georgia Infantry).

Grubb's Hussars (Company F, Cavalry Battalion, Cobb's Legion, Georgia).

Gwinnett Artillery (Company D, 9th Battalion, Georgia Artillery).

Gwinnett Cavalry (No. 1) (Company C, 10th Georgia State Guards).

Gwinnett Cavalry (No. 2) (Company H, 10th Georgia State Guards).

Gwinnett Greys (Company E, 8th Georgia State Guards).
Gwinnett Guards (Company C, 8th Georgia State Guards).
Habersham Defenders (Company D, Whitehead's Battalion, Local Defense Troops, Georgia).
Had's Partisan Rangers (Unattached Company —).
Hall Chattahoochee Cavalry (Company B. Blue Ridge Tiger Regiment, 4th Georgia State Guards).
Hall County Cavalry (Company A, Blue Ridge Tiger Regiment, 4th Georgia State Guards).
Hall Troopers (Company I, Blue Ridge Tiger Regiment, 4th Georgia State Guards).
Hall Volunteers (Company D, 55th Georgia Infantry).
Hamilton Battery (Also called Georgia Regulars, originally Company A, 1st Georgia Regulars; afterwards Independent Company, Georgia Artillery).
Hamilton Rangers (Company K, 48th Georgia Infantry).
Haralson Brown Guards (Company A, 35th Georgia Infantry).
Haralson Cavalry (Company E, McDonald's Battalion, Local Defense Troops, Georgia).
Hardee Rifles (Company H, 5th Georgia Infantry).
Hardee Rifles (Captain John L. Hardee's Company, Local Defense Troops, Georgia).
Hardwick Mounted Rifles (Company H, 7th Georgia Cavalry).
Hargett Infantry (Company F, 5th Georgia State Guards).
Harris Dragoons (Company F, 12th Georgia State Guards).
Harris Guards (Company —, Georgia —).
Harrison Volunteers (Company G, 51st Georgia Volunteers).
Hartwell Infantry (Company C, 16th Georgia Infantry).
Hawkinsville Rangers (Company B, 19th Battalion, Georgia Cavalry).
Heard Independent Cavalry (Company E, 10th Georgia State Guards).
Henry County Cavalry (Company B, 10th Georgia State Guards).
Henry County Dragoons (Company F, 10th Georgia State Guards).
Henry Guards (Company G, 19th Georgia Infantry).
Henry Infantry (Company K, 8th Georgia State Guards).
Henry Light Infantry (Company E, 25th Georgia Infantry).
High Shoals Defenders (Captain A. J. Medlin's Company, Six Months' Local Defense Troops, Georgia).
Highland Rangers (Company G, 1st Georgia Cavalry).
Hillyer Rifles (Company C, 9th Georgia Infantry).
Holloway Greys (Captain A. J. White's Company, Georgia —).
Home Guards (Company D, 3d Georgia Infantry).
Homer Cavalry (Company F, Blue Ridge Tiger Regiment, 4th Georgia State Guards).

Homer Troopers (Company A, 30th Battalion, Georgia Cavalry).

Hood's Cavalry (Company D, 29th Battalion, Georgia Cavalry).

Hook and Ladder Guard (Company D, Atlanta Fire Battalion, Local Defense Troops, Georgia).

Hopkins Partisan Rangers (Company A, 24th Battalion, Georgia Cavalry).

Hopkins Partisan Rangers (Company C, 24th Battalion, Georgia Cavalry).

Houston Guard (Company A, 8th Battalion, Georgia State Guard).

Houston Volunteers (Company K, 11th Georgia Infantry).

Huguenin Rifles (Company D, 30th Georgia Infantry).

Hunter Guards (Company C, 30th Georgia Infantry).

Hunter Rifles (Company —. 4th Georgia Infantry).

Hurt Light Artillery (Lieutenant Joseph A. Alexander's Company, Georgia Artillery).

Hunchins Guard (Captain — Thomas's Company, Georgia Volunteers).

Independent Blues (Company D, 10th Georgia Infantry).

Independent Georgia Volunteers (Captain G. W. Lee's Company, Georgia Vounteers).

Independent Volunteers (Lieutenant James A. Damour's Company, Georgia Volunteers).

Independent Volunteers (Company A, 1st Confederate Georgia).

Independent Volunteers (Company E, 9th Battalion, Georgia State Guard).

Invincibles (Captain — Holmes' Company, Georgia Volunteers).

Irish Jasper Greens (Company A, 1st Volunteers, Georgia).

Irish Volunteer Guards (Company —, 8th Georgia Infantry, 1st Volunteers Georgia).

Irish Volunteers (Company A, Company D, 1st Georgia Volunteers).

Irish Volunteers Co. B (Company E, 1st Volunteers, Georgia).

Irwin Guard (Company A, 9th Georgia Infantry).

Irwin Artillery (Originally Company A, 9th Georgia Infantry; afterward Company C. Sumter 11th Battalion, Georgia Artillery).

Irwin Invincibles (Company E. 25th Georgia Infantry).

Irwin Volunteers (20th Georgia Infantry).

Irwin Volunteers (Company F, 49th Georgia Infantry).

Ivey Guards (Company G, 20th Georgia Infantry).

Ivey Guards (Company B, 5th Georgia State Guard).

Jack Brown's (Company H. 59th Georgia Infantry).

Jackson Artillery (Captain George A. Dure's Company, Georgia Artillery).

144

Jackson Avengers (Captain — Bradford's Company, Georgia —).

Jackson Avengers (Company G, 55th Georgia Infantry).

Jackson Blues (Company B, 2d Georgia Infantry).

Jackson Cavalry (Company K, Blue Ridge Tiger Regiment, 4th Georgia State Guards).

Jackson Guards (Company B, 59th Georgia Infantry).

Jackson Mounted Guards (Company I, 9th Georgia State Guards).

Jasper Maxey Infantry (Company C, 6th Georgia State Guard).

Jeff's Cavalry (Captain H. G. Wright's Company, Local Defense Troops, Georgia).

Jefferson Guards (Company C, 20th Georgia Infantry).

Jefferson Volunteers (Company E, 48th Georgia Infantry).

Jennings Rangers (Company C, 20th Battalion, Georgia Cavalry).

Joe Brown Guard (Captain A. J. Smith's Company, Wilson's Battalion, Local Defense Troops, Georgia).

Joe Brown Rifles (Company G, Blue Ridge Tiger Regiment, 4th Georgia State Guards).

Joe Brown's, The (Company —, 2d Georgia —).

Joe Brown's Guards (Company F, 9th Georgia State Guards).

Joe Brown's Pets (Company C, 2d Georgia State Troops).

Johnson Guards (Company B, Cavalry Battalion, Phillips' Legion, Georgia Volunteers).

Jones Hussars (Captain J. J. Jones' Company, Six Months' Local Defense Troops, Georgia).

Jones State Guards (Company H, 6th Georgia State Guards).

Jones Volunteers (Company B, 12th Georgia Infantry).

Jo Thompson Artillery (Originally Company M, 38th Georgia Infantry; afterward Captain L. J. Parr's, afterward C. R. Hanleiter's Company, Georgia Artillery).

Kennesaw Guards (Company A, 7th Georgia State Guards).

LaFayette Volunteers (Company G, 9th Georgia Infantry).

LaGrange Light Guards (Company B, 4th Georgia Infantry).

Lamar Mounted Rifles (Also called Mounted Rifles, Company H, 5th Georgia Cavalry).

Lamar Rangers (Also called Mounted Rifles, Company. H, 5th Georgia Cavalry).

Lamar Infantry (Company A, 54th Georgia Infantry).

Laurens Volunteers (Company G, 49th Georgia Infantry).

Lawrenceville Infantry (Company E, 8th Georgia State Guards).

Laurens Reserves (Captain R. A. Stanley's Company, Carswell's Battalion, Local Defense Troops, Georgia).

Lee Cavalry (Captain J. H. Allen's Cavalry, Six Months Local Defense Troops, Georgia).

Lee Guards (Company B, 51st Georgia Infantry).

Lee Riflemen (Company F, Whitehead's Battalion, Local Defense Troops, Georgia).

Lee Rifles (See Augusta Lee Rifles).

Lee Volunteers (Company B, 11th Georgia Infantry).

Lee Rangers (Company E, Provost Battalion, Local Defense Troops, Georgia).

Lee's Volunteers (Company D, 1st Battalion, Georgia Infantry).

Lester Volunteers (Company E, 14th Georgia Infantry).

Letcher Guards (Company B, 10th Georgia Infantry).

Lewis and Phillips Guards (Company C, 3d Battalion, Georgia Infantry).

Leyden Artillery (Company A, 9th Battalion, Georgia Artillery).

Liberty Company (Company A, Whitehead's Battalion, Local Defense Troops, Georgia).

Liberty Dragoons (Company B, 20th Battalion, Georgia Cavalry).

Liberty Mounted Dragoons (Company B, 20th Battalion, Georgia Cavalry).

Liberty Guards (Company D, 5th Georgia Cavalry).

Liberty Independent Troop (Company G, 5th Georgia Cavalry).

Liberty Mounted Rangers (See Liberty Dragoons).

Liberty Volunteers (Company H, afterward E, 25th Georgia Infantry).

Line Guards (Company D, Stephens' Battalion, Local Defense Troops, Georgia).

Lipscomb Volunteers (Company H, 9th Georgia State Guards).

Lochrane Guards (Company F, Infantry Battalion, Phillips' Legion, Georgia).

Lockett Volunteers (Company K, 59th Georgia Infantry).

Lowndes Mounted Infantry (Company B, 11th Georgia State Guards).

Lowndes Volunteers (Company I, 12th Georgia Infantry).

Lula Fire Company No. 3 (Company C, Atlanta Fire Battalion, Local Defense Troops, Georgia).

Lula Videttes (Company F, Atlanta Fire Battalion, Local Defense Troops, Georgia).

Lumpkin Cavalry (Captain B. H. Corbin's Company, Six Months Local Defense Troops, Georgia).

Lumpkin Guards (Company E, 30th Battalion, Georgia State Troops).

McCulloch Rifles (Company L, afterward D, 38th Georgia Infantry).

McDonald Battalion (— Battalion, Georgia State Guards).

McIntosh Cavalry (Company K, 5th Georgia Cavalry).

McIntosh County Guards (Company M, 26th Georgia Infantry).

McIntosh Guards (Company M, 26th Georgia Infantry).
McIntosh Guards (Captain — McIntosh's Company, Georgia —).
McIntosh Volunteers (Captain J. W. Boggs' Company, Georgia).
McLeod Artillery (originally Company C, 38th Georgia Infantry —Wright's Legion).
McLeod Volunteers (Company H, 48th Georgia Infantry).
Macon Battalion (Battalion Local Defense Troops, Georgia).
Macon County Volunteers (Company I, 4th Georgia Infantry).
Macon Guards (Company —, 2d Georgia Infantry).
Macon Guards (Company C, 8th Georgia Infantry).
Macon Provost Guard (Company —, — Georgia —).
Macon Volunteers (Company A, Company D, 2d Battalion, Georgia Infantry).
Macon Volunteers (Company B, Captain C. H. Freeman's Company, Macon Battalion, Local Defense Troops, Georgia).
Macon and Western Railroad Guards (Captain John S. Wise's Company, Macon Battalion, Local Defense Troops, Georgia).
Madison Greys (Company A, 16th Georgia Infantry).
Marietta Infantry (Company E, 7th Georgia State Guards).
Marion Guards (Company K, 12th Georgia Infantry).
Marion Infantry (Company H, 5th Georgia State Guards).
Marshallville Volunteers (Company —, 12th Georgia State Guards).
Maxwell Artillery (Also called Regular Light Battery, Captain J. A. Maxwell's Company, Georgia Artillery, originally Company D, 1st Georgia Regulars).
Mechanic Fire Company No. 2 (Company B, Atlanta Fire Battalion, Local Defense Troops, Georgia).
Mell Volunteers (Company D, Infantry Battalion, Cobb's Legion, Georgia Volunteers).
Mercer Artillery (Company K, 28th Battalion, Georgia Infantry).
Mercer Partisans (Company A, 24th Battalion, Georgia Cavalry).
Meriwether Volunteers (Company —, 13th Georgia Infantry).
Milledge Artillery (Captain John Milledge's (Jr.) Company, Georgia Artillery).
Milledgeville Guards (Captain Wm. Caraker's Company, Six Months Local Defense Troops, Georgia).
Millen Rifles (Company E, 8th Georgia Infantry).
Millen's Partisan Rangers (20th Battalion, Georgia Cavalry).
Miller Guard (Company D, 51st Georgia Infantry).
Miller Rangers (Company C, 21s Battalion, Georgia Cavalry).
Milton Cavalry (Company B, Cavalry Battalion, Cherokee Legion, Georgia Volunteers).

147

Milton Guards (Company B, 38th Georgia Infantry).
Mitchell Guards (Company C, 31st Georgia Infantry).
Mitchell Independents (Company F, 6th Georgia Infantry).
Mitchell Van-Guard (Company C, 51st Georgia Infantry).
Mitchell Volunteer Guards (Company A, 47th Georgia Infantry).
Monroe Crowders (Company D, 31st Georgia Infantry).
Monroe Infantry (Company D, 8th Georgia State Guards).
Montgomery Artillery (14th Battalion, Georgia Artillery).
Montgomery Guards (Guilmartin's Company, 1st Volunteers, Georgia, afterward Company E, 22d Battalion, Georgia Siege Artillery).
Montgomery Sharpshooters (Company E, 61st Georgia Infantry).
Montgomery Volunteers (Company —, Carswell's Battalion, Local Defense Troops, Georgia).
Moughon Infantry (Company D, 66th Georgia Infantry).
Moultrie Cavalry (Company C, 11th Georgia State Guards).
Mountain Dragoons (Company A, 23d Battalion, Georgia Infantry).
Mountain Rangers (Company E, 21st Georgia Infantry).
Mountain Tigers (Company H, 31st Georgia Infantry).
Mountaineer Riflemen (Company I, 48th Georgia Infantry).
Mountaineers (Company D, 14th Battalion, Georgia Artillery).
Mounted Infantry (Company B, 9th Battalion, Georgia State Guards).
Mounted Infantry (Captain J. J. Jones' Company, Six Months Local Defense Troops, Georgia).
Mounted Rangers (Lieutenant J. H. Sykes' Company, Georgia Cavalry).
Muckalee Guards (Company A, 12th Georgia Infantry).
Mumford Avengers (Company —, 49th Georgia Infantry).
Murphy Guards (Company A, 12th Georgia Infantry).
Murray Cavalry (Captain W. C. Asher's Independent Company, Georgia Cavalry).
Murray Rifles (Company —, Georgia —).
Muscogee Cavalry (Company —, 12th Georgia State Guards).
Muscogee Confederates (Company B, 31st Georgia Infantry).
Muscogee Factory Guards (Company —, Thompson's Battalion, Georgia Volunteers).
Muscogee Guards (Captain A. B. Thornton's Company, Six Months Local Defense Troops, Georgia).
Muscogee Light Infantry (Company B, 20th Georgia Infantry).
Muscogee Rifles (Company E, 12th Georgia Infantry).
Muscogee Rifles (Company —, — Georgia —).
Nelson Rangers (T. M. Nelson's Independent Company, Georgia

Cavalry, General S. D. Lee's Escort).

Newnan Artillery (Company A, (Hanvey's Battery) 12th Battalion, Georgia Artillery).

Newnan Guards (Company A, 1st Georgia Volunteers).

Newnan Rangers (42d Georgia Infantry).

Ochlochnee Light Infantry (Company B, 29th Georgia Infantry).

Ocmulgee Rangers (Company A, 19th Battalion, Georgia Cavalry; afterward Company F, 10th Confederate Cavalry).

Oconee Guards (Company K, 9th Georgia State Guards).

Oconee Scouts (Capt. J. S. Joyner's Company, Georgia Volunteers).

Oconee Volunteers (Captain — Thompson's Company, Georgia Volunteers).

Ogeechee Minute Men (Captain D. W. Garrison's Company, Six Months Local Defense Troops, Georgia).

Ogeechee Rifles (Company K, afterward D, 25th Georgia Infantry)

Oglethorpe Artillery (Company —, 8th Georgia Volunteers).

Oglethorpe Blues (Company —, — Georgia —).

Oglethorpe Guards (Company D, 1st Georgia Volunteers).

Oglethorpe Infantry (Company D, 1st Volunteers, Georgia).

Oglethorpe Light Artillery (Company A, 63d Georgia Infantry).

Oglethorpe Light Infantry (Company H, 1st Volunteers, Georgia).

Oglethorpe Light Infantry (Company B, 8th Georgia Infantry).

Oglethorpe Rifles (Company K, 8th Georgia Infantry).

Oglethorpe Siege Artillery Battalion (Independent Battalion, Georgia Artillery, Companies A and B—Company A became Company C (formerly Savannah Artillery) and Company B became Company D, 22d Battalion, Georgia Siege Artillery),

O. K. Rifles (Company —, 13th Georgia Infantry).

Okefenokee Rifles (Company F, afterward G, 26th Georgia Infantry).

One Company (Company G, Atlanta Fire Battalion, Local Defense Troops, Georgia).

Ordnance Guard (Local Defense Georgia Volunteers, Macon, Georgia).

Palmetto Guards (Company C, 19th Georgia Infantry).

Panola Guards (Company G, 9th Georgia Cavalry).

Panola Guards (Rifles) (Company H, 13th Georgia Infantry).

Paulding Infantry (Company K, Infantry Battalion, Floyd Legion, Georgia State Guards).

Paulding Raid Repellers (Company A, McDonald's Battalion, Local Defense Troops, Georgia).

Paulding Volunteers (Company C, 7th Georgia Infantry).

Pauline Rifles (Captain W. H. Barteley's Company, 5th Georgia State Troops).

Perry Cavalry (Company —, 12th Georgia State Guards).

Phillips Battalion (Georgia State Guards).

Phillips Legion (Georgia Volunteers).

Phoenix Battalion (Company C, 13th Battalion, Georgia Volunteers).

Phoenix Riflemen (Company —, 1st Volunteers, Georgia; afterward Company B, 63d Georgia Infantry).

Pickens Cavalry (Company D, McDonald's Battalion, Local Defense Troops, Georgia).

Pickens Raid Repellers (Company I, Cherokee Legion, Georgia Infantry).

Pierce Guards (Company I, 49th Georgia Infantry).

Pierce Mounted Volunteers (Also called Atlantic and Gulf Guards Cavalry Company attached to 26th Georgia Infantry).

Pike Infantry (Company E, 6th Georgia State Guards).

Pioneer Infantry (Company E, Augusta Fire Brigade, Local Defense Troops, Georgia).

Pirkle Rangers (Company —, Blue Ridge Tiger Regiment, 4th Georgia State Guards).

Piscola Volunteers (Company I, 26th Georgia Infantry).

Pochitla Guards (Company E, 51st Georgia Infantry).

Polk Mounted Infantry (Company H, Cavalry Battalion, Floyd Legion, Georgia State Guards).

Polk Volunteers (Company G, Infantry Battalion, Floyd Legion, Georgia State Guards).

Pond Spring Company—Cavalry—(Company E, Culberson's Battalion, Local Defense Troops, Georgia).

Poythree Volunteers (Company E, Infantry Battalion, Cobb's Legion, Georgia Volunteers).

Provost Battalion (Battalion at Macon, Georgia).

Provost Guard (Battalion at Atlanta, Georgia).

Pulaski Artillery (Company K, 10th Georgia Infantry; afterward attached as Company L or K to 1st Virginia Artillery).

Pulaski Guards (Company K, 10th Georgia Infantry; afterward attached as Company L or K to 1st Virginia Artillery).

Pulaski Blues, (Company F, 31st Georgia Infantry).

Pulaski Cavalry (Company —, Carswell's Battalion, Local Defense Troops, Georgia).

Pulaski Greys (Company K, 49th Georgia Infantry).

Pulaski Guard (Captain H. Williams' Company, Georgia Infantry).

Pulaski Volunteers (Company G, 8th Georgia Infantry).

Putnam Infantry (Company —, Georgia Infantry).

Putnam Light Infantry (Company G, 12th Georgia Infantry).

Quitman Greys (Company —, 11th Georgia Infantry).

Quitman Guards (Company K, 1st Georgia Volunteers).

Quitman Guards (Company K, 53rd Georgia Infantry).

Railroad Guards (Company —, Thompson's Battalion, Local Defense Troops, Georgia).

Railroad Guards (Captain J. J. Matthews' Company, Georgia Volunteers).

Rains Guards (Company D, Rains' Regiment, Local Defense Troops, Augusta (?), Georgia).

Ramsey Volunteers (Company K, 16th Georgia Infantry).

Randolph Cavalry (Company A, 2d Georgia Cavalry).

Randolph Rangers (Company B, 24th Battalion, Georgia Cavalry).

Randolph Rangers (Company G, 51st Georgia Infantry).

Randolph Volunteers (Company —, 13th Georgia Infantry).

Rattlesnake Rangers (Company C, 19th Battalion, Georgia Cavalry).

Rebel Rangers (Company D, 2d Georgia State Guards).

Reese Guards (Company B, 9th Georgia State Guards).

Reids' Guards (Company C, 39th Battalion, Georgia State Troops).

Republican Blues (Originally a Battalion of Georgia Militia; afterward Companies B and C 1st Volunteers, Georgia Infantry).

Reserve Chatham Artillery (Georgia Artillery).

Richmond Dragoons (Company K, Cavalry Battalion, Cobb's Legion, Georgia Volunteers).

Richmond Hussars (Company A, Cavalry Battalion, Cobb's Legion, afterward 9th Georgia Cavalry).

Richmond Light Infantry (Company D, Augusta Fire Battalion, Local Defense Troops, Georgia).

Rigdon Guards (Captain A. J. Smith's Company, Local Defense Troops, Georgia).

Ringgold Rangers (Company C, 13th Georgia Infantry).

Ringgold Guard (Georgia).

Ringgold Rangers (Captain A. C. Bradshaw's Company (Independent) Georgia Cavalry).

Ringgold Volunteers (Company B, 1st Battalion, Georgia Infantry).

Rome Cavalry (Company C, Cavalry Battalion, Floyd Legion. Georgia State Guards).

Rome Guards (Company A, Infantry Battalion, Floyd Legion, Georgia State Guards).

Rome Light Guards (Company A, 8th Georgia Infantry).

Roswell Battalion (Cavalry) Local Defense Troops, Georgia).

Roswell Troopers (Company —, Cavalry Battalion, Cobb's Legion, Georgia .Volunteers), afterward Company E, 9th Georgia Cavalry).

Rough and Ready Boys (Captain —, Richards' Company, Georgia Volunteers).

Rough and Ready Boys (Captain —, McRae's Company, Georgia Volunteers).

Rough and Ready Volunteers (Company G, 7th Georgia State Guards).

Rowan Partisan Rangers (Company K, 6th Georgia Cavalry).

Rutland Guards (Company B, 27th Georgia Infantry).

Rutledge Sharpshooters (Company —, Georgia).

Sallacoa Silver Greys (Company F, Infantry Battalion, Cherokee Legion, Georgia Volunteers).

Sallie Twiggs Regiment (16th Georgia Infantry).

Sardis Volunteers (Company E, 21st Georgia Artillery).

Satilla Rangers (Company A, 50th Georgia Infantry).

Savannah Artillery (Captain J. B. Gallie's Company Georgia Artillery, originally attached to 1st Volunteers, Georgia Infantry).

Savannah Cadets (Company —, Georgia —).

Savannah City Light Guard (Also called City Light Guard, Company D, 1st Volunteers, Georgia Infantry).

Savannah Guards (18th Battalion Georgia Infantry).

Savannah Volunteers (18th Battalion, Georgia Infantry).

Savannah Volunteer Guards (18th Battalion, Georgia Infantry).

Savannah Volunteer Guards (A company of boys (Captain W. G. Charlton's Company, Georgia Volunteers).

Savannah River Guards (Company K, — Georgia).

Schley Cavalry (Company D, 29th Battalion, Georgia Cavalry).

Schley Riflemen (Company A, 22d Georgia Infantry).

Schley Volunteers (Company B, 17th Georgia Infantry).

Scott Infantry (Company B, 64th Georgia Infantry).

Screven Cavalry (Company —, Wright's Battalion, Local Defense Troops, Georgia).

Screven Guards (Company D, 45th Georgia Infantry).

Screven Troop (Company B, 2d Battalion, Georgia Cavalry).

Seaboard Guards (Company C, 26th Georgia Infantry).

Second Independent Battalion Infantry (Georgia Volunteers).

Semmes Guard (Company C, 2d Georgia Infantry).

"Seventeenth" Patriots (Company K, 29th Georgia Infantry).

Shiloh Troop (Company K, 4th (Clinch's) Georgia Cavalry).

Sidney Johnstons (Company G, 59th Georgia Infantry).

Silver Greys (afterward called Bibb Greys (Company A, Rains' Regiment, Local Defense Troops, Georgia).

Slappey Guards (Company G, 48th Georgia Infantry).

Slocomb Volunteers (Company B, Whitehead's Battalion, Local Defense Troops, Georgia).

Sons of Dixie (Company G, 20th Georgia Infantry).

Southern Guards (Company B, 1st Georgia Volunteers).

Southern Guards (Company G,) (Company I, 20th Georgia Infantry).

Southern Rifles (Company A, 4th Georgia Infantry).

Southern Rights Battery (Company A, 14th Battalion, Georgia Artillery).

Southern Rights Guards (Company C, 1st Georgia Volunteers).

Southern Rights Volunteers (Company A, 25th Georgia Infantry).

Southwestern Railroad Guards (Captain J. M. Walden's Company, Macon Battalion, Local Defense Troops, Georgia).

Southwestern Railroad Infantry (Captain C. D. Wall's Company, Macon Battalion, Local Defense Troops, Georgia).

Spalding Greys (Company B, 2d Independent Battalion, Georgia Infantry).

Spalding Infantry (Company I, 6th Georgia State Guards).

Spalding Volunteers (Company K, 6th Georgia State Guards).

Stark Guards (Company F, 61st Georgia Infantry).

Stark Volunteers (Company I, 13th Georgia Infantry).

State Armory Guards (Captain J. W. Green's Company, Six Months Local Defense Troops, Georgia).

State Rights Guards (Company E, 49th Georgia Infantry).

Stephens Battalion (Battalion Georgia State Guards).

Stephens Home Guard (Company D, 15th Georgia Infantry).

Stephens Light Artillery (Georgia Artillery; prior to November 1863, 3d Maryland Battery).

Stephens Light Guard (Company I, 8th Georgia Infantry).

Stephens Rifles (Company C, 9th Georgia Cavalry).

Stephens Volunteers (Company G, 29th Georgia Infantry).

Stewart Greys (Company K, 2d Georgia Infantry).

Stewart Infantry (Company —, Yarborough's Battalion, Local Defense Troops, Georgia).

Stewart Infantry (Company I, 21st Georgia Infantry).

Stone Mountain Guards (Company H, 8th Georgia State Guards).

Stonewall Cavalry (Company —, 12th Georgia State Guards).

Stonewall Guards (Company D, 6th Georgia State Guards).

Stonewall Hussars Lieutenant J. D. Harrell's Company, Georgia Volunteers).

Stonewall Volunteers (Company A, 5th Georgia State Guards).

Sulphur Spring Guard (Company B, 2d Georgia State Guard).

Sumter Battalion (11th Battalion Georgia Artillery).

Sumter Cavalry (Company —, 12th Georgia State Guards).

Sumter Flying Artillery (Captain A. S. Cutts' Company, Georgia Artillery; afterward Company A, 11th Battalion Georgia Artillery).

Sumter Light Guards (Company K, 4th Georgia Infantry).

Swamp Rangers (Company D, 19th Battalion, Georgia Cavalry).

Sydney Brown Infantry (Captain —, Arnold's Company Georgia Volunteers).

Talbot Guards (Company E, 9th Georgia Infantry).

Talbot Infantry (Company F, 5th Georgia State Guards).

Talbot Troopers (Company —, 12th Georgia State Guards).

Taliaferro Volunteers (Company D, 49th Georgia Infantry).

Tattnall Invincibles (Company G, 47th Georgia Infantry).

Tattnall Rangers (Company B, 61st Georgia Infantry).

Tattnall Guards (Company G, 1st Volunteers, Georgia Infantry).

Taylor Cavalry (Company —, 12th Georgia State Guards).

Taylor Infantry (Company K, 5th Georgia State Guards).

Telfair Irish Greys (Company A, 25th Georgia Infantry).

Telfair Volunteers (Company B, 48th Georgia Infantry).

Telfair Volunteers (Company H, 20th Georgia Infantry.

Terrell Infantry (Company F, 51st Georgia Infantry).

Terrell Light Artillery (Captain E. G. Dawson's Company, Georgia Artillery).

Thomas Cavalry (Company A, 11th Georgia State Guards).

Thomas County Rangers (Company E, 50th Georgia Infantry).

Thomas County Volunteers (Company H, 29th Georgia Infantry).

Thomas Legion (Georgia Volunteers).

Thomas Reserves (Captain A. H. Hamell's (Hahsell's) Company, Georgia Volunteers).

Thomasville Guards (Company A, 29th Georgia Infantry).

Thompson Guard, 7th Battalion Georgia).

Thompson Guards (Company F, 10th Georgia Infantry).

Thompson Guards (Company —, 13th Georgia —).

Thompson Guards (Company I, 61st Georgia Infantry).

Thompson Rangers (Company D, 2d Georgia Infantry).

Tilton Volunteers (Company B, 1st Georgia State Guards).

Toccoa Infantry (Company G, Whitehead's Battalion, Local Defense Troops, Georgia).

Tom Cobb Infantry (Company E, 38th Georgia Infantry).

Toombs Guards (Company I, 9th Georgia Infantry).

Toombs Rangers (Company D, 20th Georgia Infantry).

Toombs Rangers (Company C, 21st Georgia Infantry).

Toombs Volunteers (Company F, 4th Georgia Infantry).

Town Rangers (Company A, Cavalry Battalion, Smith's Legion, Georgia Volunteers).

Troup Artillery (Originally attached to 2d Georgia Infantry,

afterward Company A, Cobb's Legion, afterward Captain
M. Stanley's Independent Company Georgia Artillery).

Tugalo Rangers (Company D, 30th Battalion, Georgia Cavalry).

Turner Guards (Company I, 59th Georgia Infantry).

Twiggs Cavalry (Company —, Carswell's Battalion, Local Defense Troops, Georgia).)

Twiggs Guards (Company I, 6th Georgia Infantry).

Twiggs Volunteers (Company C, 4th Georgia Infantry).

Valdosta Guards (Company D, 50th Georgia Infantry).

Valley Rangers (Company D, — Georgia —).

Vason Guards (Captain P. Robinson's Company, Georgia Volunteers).

Vigilant Infantry (Company A, Augusta Fire Brigade, Local Defense Troops, Georgia).

Walker Cavalry (Company A, Culberson's Battalion, Local Defense Troops, Georgia).

Walker Cavalry (Company B, Culberson's Battalion, Local Defense Troops, Georgia).

Walker Cavalry (Company C, Culberson's Battalion, Local Defense Troops, Georgia).

Walker Independents (Company C, 60th Georgia Infantry).

Walker Light Infantry (Company I, 1st Georgia Volunteers).

Walker Rifles (Company E, 55th Georgia Infantry).

Walton Guards (Company E, 9th Georgia State Guards).

Walton Infantry (Company H, 11th Georgia Infantry).

Walton Rangers (Company —, 10th Georgia State Guards).

War Department Guards (Company A, 3d Battalion. Local Defense Troops, Georgia).

Ward Volunteers (Company C, 9th Georgia State Guards).

Ware Guards (Company D, 26th Georgia Infantry).

Ware Volunteers (Company B, 50th Georgia Infantry).

Ware Volunteers (Company —, 11th Georgia State Guards).

Warren Akin Guards (Company E, 64th Georgia Infantry).

Warren Defenders (Company —, Wilson's Battalion, Local Defense Troops, Georgia).

Warren Infantry (Company B, 48th Georgia Infantry).

Warsaw Rifles (Company C, 25th Georgia Infantry).

Washington Artillery (Assigned as Company F to 1st Independent Battalion, afterward Company F, 1st Confederate Volunteers, 36th Georgia Infantry; afterward Burtwell's and Pritchard's Batteries).

Washington County Company (Company E, 1st Georgia Volunteers).

Washington Guards (Company C, 49th Georgia Infantry).

Washington Light Infantry (Company B, Augusta Fire Battalion, Local Defense Troops, Georgia).

Washington Rifles (Company B, 32d Georgia Infantry).

Washington Rifles (Company E, 1st Georgia Volunteers).

Washington Volunteers (Company K, 1st Volunteers, Georgia Infantry).

Wayne Cavalry Guards (Company Six Months Local Defense Troops, Georgia).

Wayne Guards (Company G, 6th Georgia State Guards).

Wayne & Mercer Rangers (Company A, 24th Battalion, Georgia Cavalry).

Wayne Rangers (Company A, 4th (Clinch's Georgia Cavalry).

Wayne Rangers (Company A, 24th Battalion, Georgia Cavalry).

Webster Invincibles (46th Georgia Infantry).

Webster Rifles (Company A, 17th Georgia Infantry).

West Infantry (Company E, Whitehead's Battalion, Local Defense Troops, Georgia).

West Point Guards (Company D, 4th Georgia Infantry).

Western & Atlantic Guards (Captain — Hull's Company, Georgia Infantry).

White Home Guards (Company G, 8th Georgia State Guards).

Whitesville Guards (Company E, 20th Georgia Infantry).

Whitfield Volunteers (Company D, 60th Georgia Infantry).

Whittle Guards (Company D, 10th Battalion, Georgia Infantry).

Wilcox Cavalry Greys (Company —, Carswell's Battalion, Local Defense Troops, Georgia).

Wilcox Rifles (Company H, 10th Georgia Infantry).

Wilkerson Rifles (Company F, 3d Georgia Infantry).

Wilkinson Invincibles (Company A, 49th Georgia Infantry).

Wilkinson Volunteers (Company O, Carswell's Battalion, Local Defense Troops, Georgia).

Wilkinson Volunteers (Company A, 6th Georgia State Guards).

Williams Volunteers (Company C, 32d Georgia Infantry),

Wilson Tigers (Company I, 48th Georgia Infantry).

Wiregrass Boys (Company A, 20th Battalion, Georgia Cavalry).

Wiregrass Minutemen (Company C, 26th Georgia Infantry).

Wiregrass Rifle Company (Company F, 26th Georgia Infantry).

Worth Infantry (Company F, 59th Georgia Infantry).

Worth Reserves (Company Six Months Local Defense Troops, Georgia).

Wright Infantry (Company H, 2d Georgia Infantry).

Wright's Legion (38th Georgia Infantry).

Yancey Invincibles (Company H, 21st Georgia Infantry).

Young Guards (Company A, 3d Georgia Infantry).

Zollicoffer Riflemen (Company C, 10th Battalion, Georgia Infantry).

INDEX.

159

163